CATALYST™
PRIME
ACCELL™
ACCELL
D0573515

CATALYST™
PRIME
ACCELL™

"HOME SCHOOLING"

WRITTEN BY **JOE CASEY**
PENCILED BY **DAMION SCOTT**
INKED BY **ROBERT CAMPANELLA** WITH **MOSH STUDIOS**
LETTERED BY **AW DESIGNS' DC HOPKINS**
COLORED BY **SIGMUND TORRE**
SPECIAL THANKS TO **RAMÓN GOVEA**

"THE EVENT"

WRITTEN BY **PRIEST** AND **JOSEPH PHILLIP ILLIDGE**
ILLUSTRATED BY **MARCO TURINI** AND **WILL ROSADO**
LETTERED BY **ANDWORLD DESIGN**
COLORED BY **JESSICA KHOLINNE**

JOSEPH ILLIDGE - SENIOR EDITOR
DESIREE RODRIGUEZ - EDITORIAL ASSISTANT

COVER BY **DAMION SCOTT**

Publisher's Cataloging-In-Publication Data

(Prepared by The Donohue Group, Inc.)

Names: Illidge, Joseph, editor. | Rodriguez, Desiree, editor.

Title: Accell. Vol. 1 / Joseph Illidge - Senior Editor ; Desiree Rodriguez - Editorial Assistant ; cover by Damion Scott.

Other Titles: Catalyst Prime

Description: [St. Louis, Missouri] : The Lion Forge, LLC, 2017. | "Portions of this book were previously published in Accell Vol. 1, Issues 1-4 and FCBD 2017 Catalyst Prime: The Event."

Identifiers: ISBN 978-1-941302-37-8

Subjects: LCSH: Superheroes--California--Los Angeles--Comic books, strips, etc. | Mexican Americans--California--Los Angeles--Comic books, strips, etc. | Speed--Comic books, strips, etc. | LCGFT: Graphic novels.

Classification: LCC PN6728 .A33 2017 | DDC 741.5973--dc23

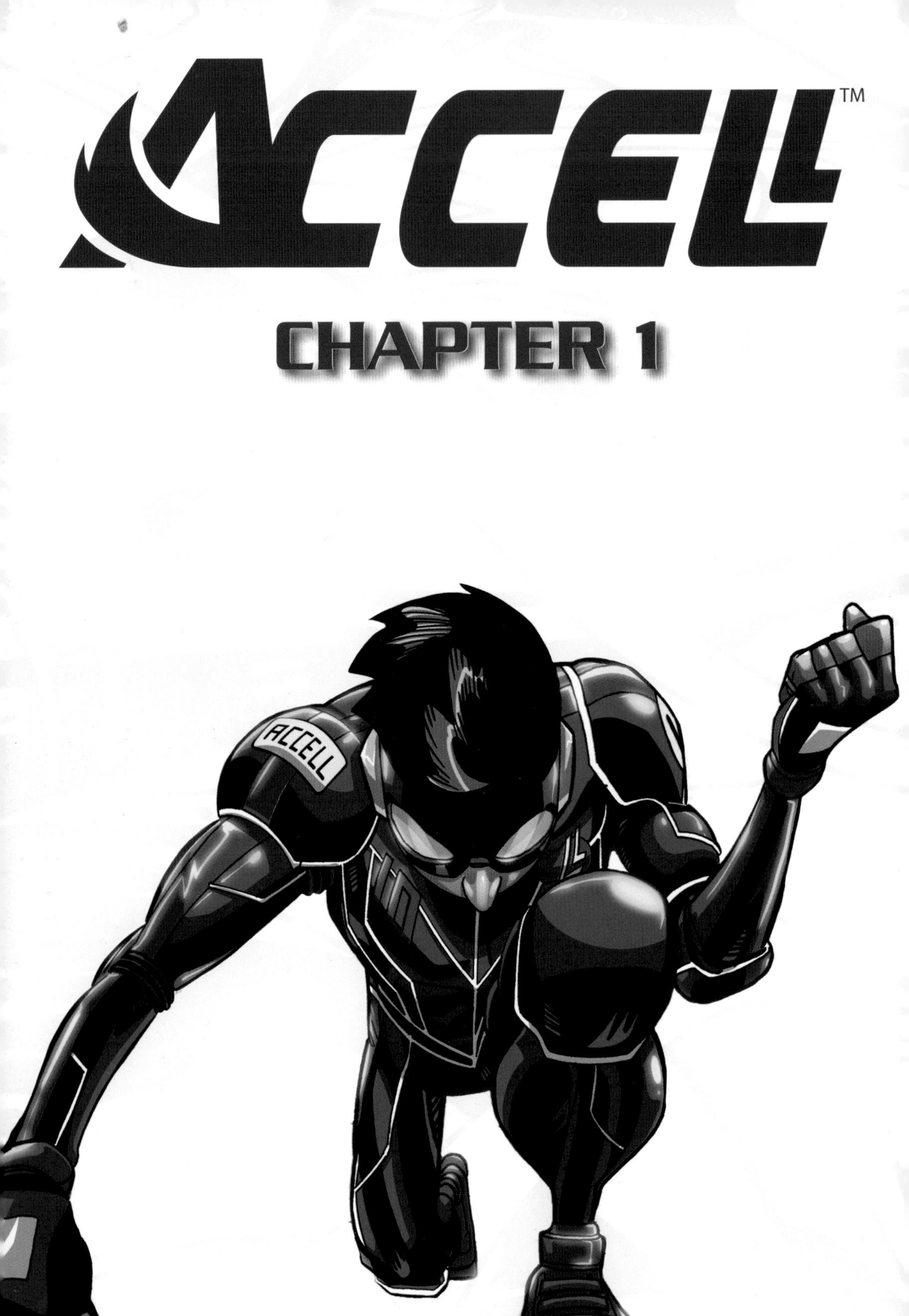
ACCELL™
CHAPTER 1
ACCELL

SO, YEAH... MY NAME'S DANIEL DOS SANTOS. I'M TWENTY YEARS YOUNG AND THIS IS MY LIFE UP IN HERE.
AT THIS PARTICULAR MOMENT, I'M WHIPPING SOME ASS ON CAR JACK CITY 2. PLAYING ONLINE MEANS I GET TO TRASH TALK PIMPLY-FACED PUNKS ALL OVER THE WORLD FROM THE COMFORT OF MY OWN CRIB. GOOD TIMES.
THERE'S SOMETHING ELSE ABOUT ME, TOO...BUT THAT'LL HAVE TO WAIT. I'M A LITTLE BUSY RIGHT NOW...
HIYO! HERE WE GO--!
UH OH... IT'S ALL GOING DOWN NOW...
THINK YOU PARKED IN A RED ZONE, BABY!
STAY AWAY FROM MY RIDE, YO--!
RAT BIKES
BONA PIZZERIA
FRESH
GRAB YOUR KICKS AND DIG THIS--
17:13
$00287881
10
100
--THAT'S WHAT I'M TALKIN' ABOUT!
YO YO YO! WHAT'S UP WITH THAT?!
COLD BLOODED...
HEY, DOS SANTOS! YOU IN L.A., RIGHT?
YEAH. SO...?
SOME TERRORIST-STYLE ACTION HAPPENING THERE! CHECK IT OUT--
OKAY, HOLD ON...

--THIS LIVE SHOT OF THE HIJACKED PRIVATE PLANE ENTERING DOWNTOWN AIRSPACE RIGHT NOW!
AIR SUPPORT IS EN ROUTE FROM EDWARDS, BUT IT'S UNCERTAIN WHETHER OR NOT THEY CAN ARRIVE IN TIME TO PREVENT THE HIJACKER'S OBJECTIVE..
LIVE SHOT - ACTION NEWS 5 - LIVE SHOT - ACTION NEW
ARRIVE IN TIME?! THEY GOTTA' BE KIDDING ME--
SEE, HERE'S THE THING ABOUT ME...
HEY--
THAT'S--
WHAT--
--MAN!
--ARE YOU DOING OVER THERE?!
--MESSED UP!
--NO WORRIES, Y'ALL!
...I'M ALSO FASTER THAN THE SPEED OF THOUGHT!
VAM
NOW, BEAR WITH ME. I'M STILL KINDA' NEW AT THIS.
LET'S GET MOVING!

THEY SAY SPEED IS RELATIVE...
1500
2500
3000
MPH
SOMETIMES IT'S HARD TO TELL IF I'M MOVING FAST...OR IF THE REST OF THE WORLD HAS JUST STOPPED...
WHATEVER. I'M ALL ABOUT DOING THE RIGHT THING.
AND THIS BIRD'S ABOUT THREE SECONDS AWAY FROM PLOWING FULL-TILT INTO AN UNSUSPECTING SKYSCRAPER...!

ONE OF THE FIRST THINGS I DISCOVERED ABOUT WHAT I CAN DO... WHEN I'M AT TOP SPEED, THERE'S NO SOUND...
...NOTHING BUT SILENCE ALL AROUND ME. NOT ONLY THAT (AND THIS IS THE BEST PART)...
...I CAN'T FEEL ANYTHING EITHER.
MAKES AN ENTRANCE LIKE THIS A LOT MORE DOABLE.
PERFECT. JUST THREE SUITS WHO HAD NO IDEA THEIR BUSINESS CHARTER WAS GONNA TURN KAMIKAZE--
--I GOT 'EM ALL IN ONE SCOOP.
GOTTA TIME MY LANDING JUST RIGHT THOUGH--

--MAKE SURE THESE GUYS DON'T SUFFER ANY RUG BURNS.
I'M SURE THEY'LL BE FINE.
I-I DON'T KNOW WHAT HAS HAPPENED TO THIS AIRCRAFT--
--BUT I WILL NOT BE DETERRED!
THE AMERICAN DISSENTION MOVEMENT WILL BE HEARD! LET THIS ACT OF SELF-SACRIFICE SERVE AS A WARNING TO ALL THOSE WHO--
ACCELL
BLAH, BLAH, BLAH...

LUCKILY, THERE'S A FEDERAL BUILDING RIGHT ON TEMPLE --
--SOMEONE THERE'LL KNOW WHAT TO DO WITH THIS NUTJOB.
NOW COMES THE HARD PART. THE ADRENALINE STARTS WEARING OFF...
...I START TO HEAR THINGS, LIKE MY OWN HEARTBEAT. AND I KNOW I'VE ONLY GOT SECONDS TO MAKE IT--
GENERAL HOSPITAL
--BEFORE THE ABUSE I JUST PUT MY BODY THROUGH FINALLY CATCHES UP WITH ME.
WHOA!
WHAT THE HELL--?!

H-HEY... WASSUP...?
THINK... YOU GUYS...CAN HELP A BRUTHA OUT...
...MAYBE A BED... OR SOMETHING--
--*
YEAH. THAT'S THE COST OF DOING BUSINESS...
...BUT, Y'KNOW, THERE ARE SOME PERKS.
DANNY...?
DID YOU JUST SAY SOMETHING...?
OMIGOD-- YOU'RE AWAKE!
Y-YEAH...
...I... GUESS SO...
BY THE WAY, THAT'S MY CURRENT PRINCESA, MONICA HAYES.
SO, ANYWAY, SMASHING THOUGH THE METAL HULL OF A PLANE A COUPLE OF TIMES WILL DO SOME SERIOUS DAMAGE TO THE HUMAN BODY...

...BUT DON'T WORRY. I'VE BEEN HERE BEFORE. I KNOW EXACTLY HOW THIS PLAYS OUT.
OKAY, HOW'RE WE DOING IN HERE...?
DOCTOR! HE JUST OPENED HIS EYES!
WELL, THAT'S SURPRISING, CONSIDERING THE BROKEN BONES, MULTIPLE LACERATIONS... SOME POSSIBLE BRAIN DAMAGE, EVEN.
WHAT, DID YOU BASH YOUR HEAD AGAINST A STEEL WALL OR SOMETHING...?
I'D LIKE TO SCHEDULE ANOTHER FULL BODY SCAN, MISTER DOS SANTOS--
F-FORGET IT, DOC...
...IT AIN'T... NECESSARY...
JUST... GIMME A QUICK SECOND...
WELL, I'M NOT SURE WHAT YOURRRRrrrr...
SHOULD HE EVEN BEEEeeee...
SO I LEARNED THIS TRICK EARLY ON...
... I DON'T HAVE TO BE RUNNING TO SPEED MYSELF UP.
NORMALLY, IT MIGHT TAKE SOMEONE MONTHS TO HEAL FROM THESE KINDS OF INJURIES...

R
E
...BUT MY BODY CAN WORK ON A SLIGHTLY DIFFERENT SCHEDULE.
DON'T ASK ME THE SCIENCE BEHIND IT...LET'S JUST SAY I CAN SPEED UP THE HEALING PROCESS WHEN I NEED TO.
PRETTY COOL, HUH?
RRRRRR ULTIMATE PROGNOSIS IS, UNTIL WE--
EEEEE TRYING TO TALK--
HEY, GUYS...
...NOT TO DERAIL THE DISCUSSION, BUT I'M FEELING MUCH BETTER NOW?
CAN YOU MAYBE GET ME OUT OF ALL THIS STUFF...?
IT TOOK SOME CONVINCING, BUT EVENTUALLY THEY SEE WHAT'S WHAT. AND AFTER THEY PICK THEIR JAWS UP OFF THE FLOOR, WE'RE OUTTA THERE...!
OSP
...MEAN, IT'S GOTTA BE SOME KINDA MIRACLE, DANNY...!
NOT EXACTLY, BABE. LET'S SCARF SOME PROTEIN AND I'LL TELL YOU ALL ABOUT IT...
SO, I GET THAT YOU RUN AROUND IN YOUR LITTLE OUTFIT, BUT I STILL DON'T UNDERSTAND HOW YOU--
OKAY, LEMME GIVE YOU A LITTLE BACKSTORY. I WASN'T BORN THIS WAY, Y'KNOW...

...NOW, WHAT I'M ABOUT TO TELL YOU, I'M TELLING YOU IN CONFIDENCE, A'IGHT?
DON'T GO TWEETIN' ABOUT THIS STUFF...
"...BUT YOU REMEMBER WHEN THE WORLD WAS GONNA END...ALL THOSE METEOR PIECES RAINING DOWN...AND ALL THE TROUBLE THEY CAUSED...?
"WELL, I SAW FIRST HAND THE KIND OF TROUBLE THEY COULD CAUSE...
"...NOW, AS IT TURNED OUT, INSTEAD OF TAKING OUT THE ENTIRE L.A. BASIN, THIS PIECE WAS ABOUT AS SMALL AS YOU CAN GET. LIKE, MARBLE-SIZED SMALL, Y'KNOW...?"
"SO WHAT DID YOU DO...?"
"ARE YOU KIDDING? WHAT DO YOU THINK I DID...?
"I BROUGHT IT HOME AND KEPT IT UNDER MY BED, OF COURSE! I THOUGHT THE THING MIGHT BE WORTH SOMETHING...!"

TURNS OUT, IT DISINTEGRATED ON ITS OWN AFTER ABOUT A WEEK. BUT ALL THAT TIME BEING NEAR IT...WELL, IT DID SOMETHING TO ME.
OBVIOUSLY, RIGHT?
GOD, IT'S SO WEIRD. YOU'RE LIKE... A SUPERHERO OR SOMETHING...!
NO WONDER I LOVE YOU SO MUCH!
AND THERE IT WAS...THE "L" WORD.
NOW, DON'T GET ME WRONG...MONICA'S A GREAT GAL. BUT THIS "LOVE" STUFF TENDS TO MAKE A GIRL DRAMATIC.
AND IF THERE'S ONE THING I DON'T NEED MORE OF IN MY LIFE...
...IT'S DRAMA.
"--BUT DOES SHE LISTEN TO ME...?!"
YOU GOT NO BUSINESS HANGING OUT WITH THAT SPEED FREAK! I FORBID YOU TO--
YOU CAN'T TELL ME WHO TO LOVE, DADDY!
DANIEL'S MY SOUL MATE AND THERE'S NOTHING YOU CAN DO ABOUT IT!
THAT NO-GOOD DAUGHTER OF MINE HAS GONE FROM JUST PUSHING THE OCCASIONAL BOUNDARY TO WILLFUL DEFIANCE!
I TOLD HER TO STAY AWAY FROM THAT DOS SANTOS KID--
NOTHING I CAN DO, HUH...?
WE'LL JUST SEE ABOUT THAT, WON'T WE...?

YOU'RE DOING THE RIGHT THING, MISTER HAYES.
YOU'RE DAMN RIGHT I AM! I'M A BUSINESSMAN-- I KNOW HOW TO FIGHT FIRE WITH FIRE!
YOU WANT FIRE...

...I'VE GOT FIREPOWER.
CUSTOM-MADE SELF-LOADING AUSTRIAN PFEIFER-ZELISKA .600 NITRO EXPRESS MAGNUM GAUNTLETS A.K.A. "FINGER CANNONS"
FOR THE MONEY I'M PAYING YOU, I WANT THIS LITTLE SNOT TO SUFFER.
YOU CATCH MY DRIFT...?
INDUBITABLY. TO BE HONEST, I'M EVEN LOOKING FORWARD TO IT--
--BUT DON'T WORRY. I WON'T LET MY FUN GET IN THE WAY OF THE JOB. I'M A PAIN PROFESSIONAL.
WHEN YOU HIRE
BARRAGE
TO DO YOUR DIRTY WORK FOR YOU... YOU'VE HIRED THE BEST.

SOMETHING WEIRD ABOUT MY LIFE LATELY...
...IT MOVES PRETTY FAST.
SO, MISTER DOS SANTOS... ANY MORE TRICKS YOU WANNA SHOW ME?
YOU MEAN, ASIDE FROM AVERTING DOMESTIC TERROR ATTACKS AND A SIDE ORDER OF SPEED HEALING...?
I GUESS THAT'S PRETTY GOOD. BUT WHEN DO I GET TO SEE YOU UP CLOSE IN UNIFORM...?
ONLY IF DUTY CALLS.
OKAY, OKAY. I KNOW IT'S BEEN A LONG DAY.
WE CAN GET INTO THE KINKY STUFF LATER...
NO SUCH THING AS LONG DAYS, BABY. NOT ANYMORE.
YOU'RE SO COOL.
LOVE YOU!
AND SHE THINKS I MOVE FAST...!

MY DAUGHTER IS JUST WALKING IN NOW...
...WHICH MEANS HE JUST LEFT.
I CAN HEAR THE QUIVER IN YOUR VOICE, MISTER HAYES. YOU CAN'T LET EMOTION RULE YOUR ACTIONS.
DON'T TELL ME NOT TO BE EMOTIONAL! NOT WHEN I'M FINANCING YOUR OPERATION--
--SO ARE YOU TRACKING HIM OR NOT?!
I AM. AND YOU SAID YOU WANTED HIM TO SUFFER...
...NO PROBLEM WHATSOEVER.

MAYBE I SHOULDN'T HAVE TOLD MONICA HOW I GOT THIS WAY. BUT I'M STILL IN SHOCK MYSELF...!
SEEMED PERFECTLY COOL AT THE TIME.
WHO KNEW WHAT TO EXPECT, BEING EXPOSED TO THAT METEOR CHUNK...
...I DIDN'T FEEL ANY DIFFERENT. AND THEN SOMETHING HAPPENED...
LIKE A REFLEX, BUT WITH A BIT OF ADDED SPICE--
OH DAMN--

--IT WAS LIKE EVERYTHING WAS SUDDENLY IN FREEZE FRAME AND I WAS STILL MOVING AT NORMAL SPEED.
NOW, EVEN WHEN IT'S NOT FULLY TURNED ON, I STILL SEE THE WORLD DIFFERENTLY.
LIKE REALITY IS GRADUALLY WARPING ALL AROUND ME...
...AND I'M JUST CAUGHT IN THE SLIPSTREAM.
MAKES ME WONDER HOW MUCH CONTROL I REALLY HAVE.
MAYBE WHEN IT COMES TO THESE NEW ABILITIES...I'M JUST HANGING ON BY MY--

THAT LOOKED PAINFUL.
THINK I MIGHT BE COLLECTING THE BACK HALF OF MY FEE BEFORE SUNRISE.
YOU GOT HIM?! DON'T JERK ME AROUND, BARRAGE...

...TELL ME YOU'VE ALREADY NAILED THAT LITTLE PUNK-ASS...!
DADDY...

HUH.
NOT EXACTLY.
DON'T TELL ME YOU MISSED--
--WHAT HAPPENED TO, "WHEN YOU HIRE BARRAGE... YOU'VE HIRED THE BEST?!"
FOR THE AMOUNT OF MONEY I'M SPENDING--I WANT A CONFIRMED KILL, YOU HEAR ME?!
WHAT DID I TELL YOU ABOUT EMOTIONS, MISTER HAYES...?
DON'T LECTURE ME, YOU FREAK!
"FREAK"? STICKS AND STONES WILL--
--HUNNNDD--!
ACCELL

OKAY, THIS GUY'S TOTALLY TRICKED OUT...
YOU LOOKING FOR A HALLOWEEN PARTY, PAL? YOU'RE A FEW MONTHS OFF--
ACCEL
--OR MAYBE YOU'RE JUST ON YOUR WAY TO WEST HOLLYWOOD...
LOOK WHO'S TALKING, KID...
...NOW STAND STILL!
"STAND STILL"? THESE DAYS, I DON'T KNOW THE MEANING OF THAT PHRASE.
YEAH.
I'LL JUST STAND HERE.
AND LET YOU NAIL ME.
SURE.
THAT'LL HAPPEN.
RIGHT.
GOOD THING I CAME PREPARED...

...TO DEAL WITH YOUR PARTICULAR TALENTS.
MOTION SENSORS: ACTIVE////// TRACKING SIGNAL////// TARGETING --
I'M THE REAL DEAL!
I POUR ON THE SPEED...SO I'M JUST GRAZED...
BUT I'M DEFINITELY GONNA FEEL THAT LATER...
...SO THIS GUY MEANS BUSINESS.
NOW YOU'RE STARTING TO GET IT.
I'M NOT JUST OUT LOOKING FOR A GOOD TIME--
HE TALKS WAY TOO MUCH.

I'M HOPING THIS SHUTS HIS PIE HOLE. OTHERWISE, I CAN'T PREDICT WHAT COULD--
GYYUHHH--!
OUCH.
NEVER MIND...
ACCELL
NOTHING LIKE A GOOD, OL' FASHIONED STREET FIGHT--
--DON'TCHA THINK?!
ACCELL
YOU NEED MORE THAN QUICK FEET AND AN ATTITUDE TO MAKE IT IN THIS BUSINESS.
THERE'S NOT THAT MANY OF US...BUT WE MAKE IT COUNT.

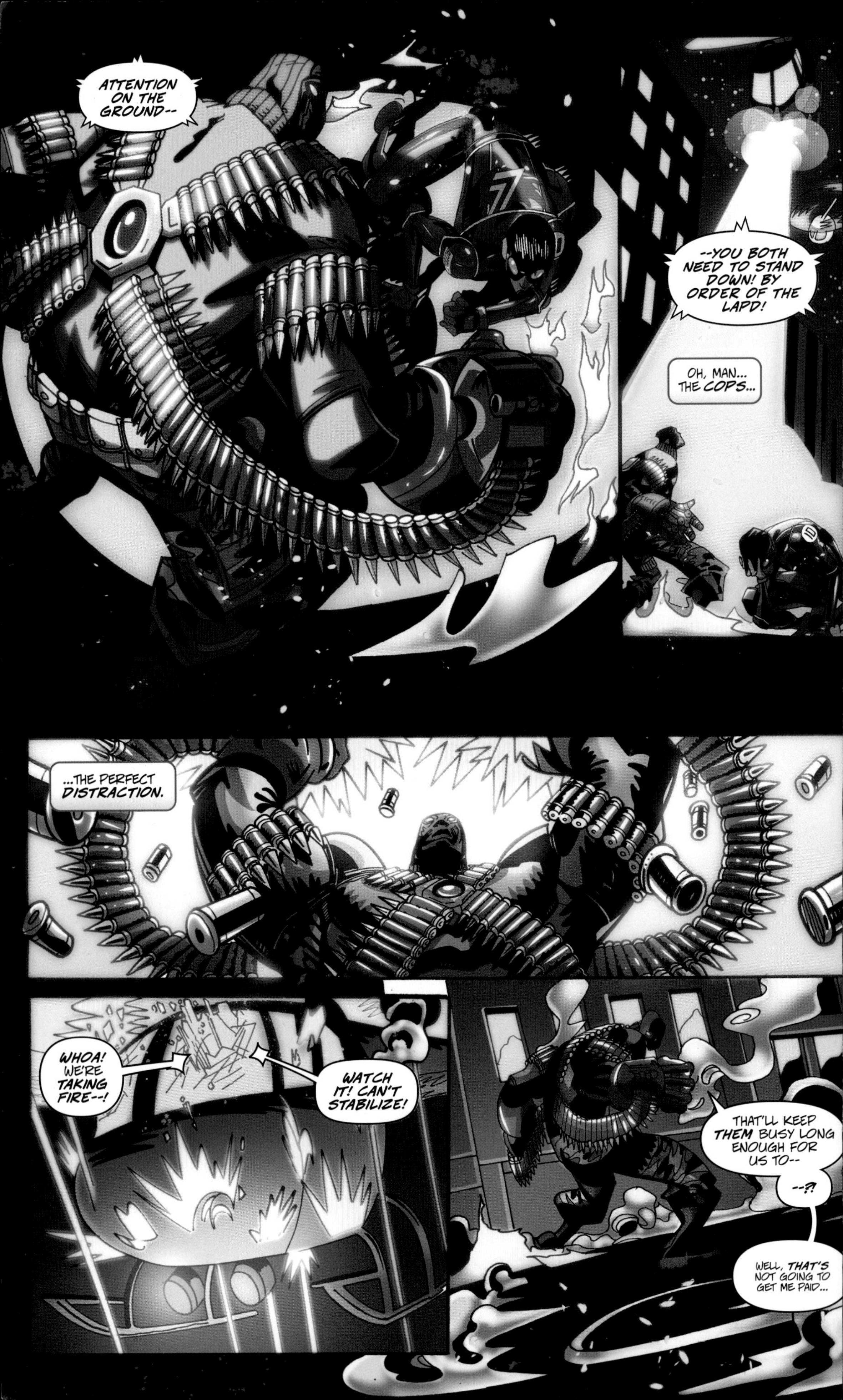
ATTENTION ON THE GROUND--
--YOU BOTH NEED TO STAND DOWN! BY ORDER OF THE LAPD!
OH, MAN... THE COPS...
...THE PERFECT DISTRACTION.
WHOA! WE'RE TAKING FIRE--!
WATCH IT! CAN'T STABILIZE!
THAT'LL KEEP THEM BUSY LONG ENOUGH FOR US TO--
--?!
WELL, THAT'S NOT GOING TO GET ME PAID...

DANNY...!
...ALL-OUT WAR ERUPTING ON WILSHIRE BLVD! OUR EYEWITNESS CHOPPER CAM IS ON THE SCENE, BRINGING US THESE ARRESTING IMAGES...
...REPORTS ARE COMING IN THAT THERE ARE TWO INDIVIDUALS INVOLVED...BOTH OF THEM WEARING BIZARRE COSTUMES...
...RIGHT NOW, IT'S TOTAL CHAOS... WITH MORE POLICE RESPONDING ON THE GROUND AND IN THE AIR...
...AND, AT THE MOMENT, WE CAN'T GET A CLEAR VIEW OF EITHER INDIVIDUAL INVOLVED...
OH MY GAAWWDD--!
...THERE'S EVERY POSSIBILITY THAT WITH ALL THE SHOOTING GOING ON...ONE OR BOTH OF THEM COULD ALREADY BE DEAD...

GENERAL HOSPITAL
GENERAL HOSPI
SO...YEAH.
I'M NOT DEAD. NOT EVEN CLOSE.
IT ONLY FEELS LIKE IT...
...ANOTHER VERSE, SAME AS THE FIRST. EVEN THOUGH I DON'T FEEL THE DAMAGE I TAKE WHEN I'M MOVING, WHEN I STOP...
...IT ALL CATCHES UP WITH ME. ALL AT ONCE.
YOU BETTER BELIEVE THAT SUCKS.
I'LL DO MY SPEED HEALING MAGIC ACT IN A FEW, BUT FOR NOW I'LL TAKE ADVANTAGE OF THIS LITTLE TIME OUT AND CATCH UP ON SOME NEWS...
...IN THE AFTERMATH OF LAST NIGHT'S CONFLICT, AUTHORITIES ARE LEFT ASKING THEMSELVES...
...WHO ARE THESE MYSTERY MEN AND ARE WE EVER GOING TO SEE THEM AGAIN?
GOOD QUESTION.
ANOTHER OUTCOME LIKE THIS...AND I'LL START ASKING IT MYSELF.
MAYBE I'M NOT CUT OUT FOR THE HERO GAME. MAYBE I SHOULD JUST...CALL OFF THE WHOLE DAMN THING.

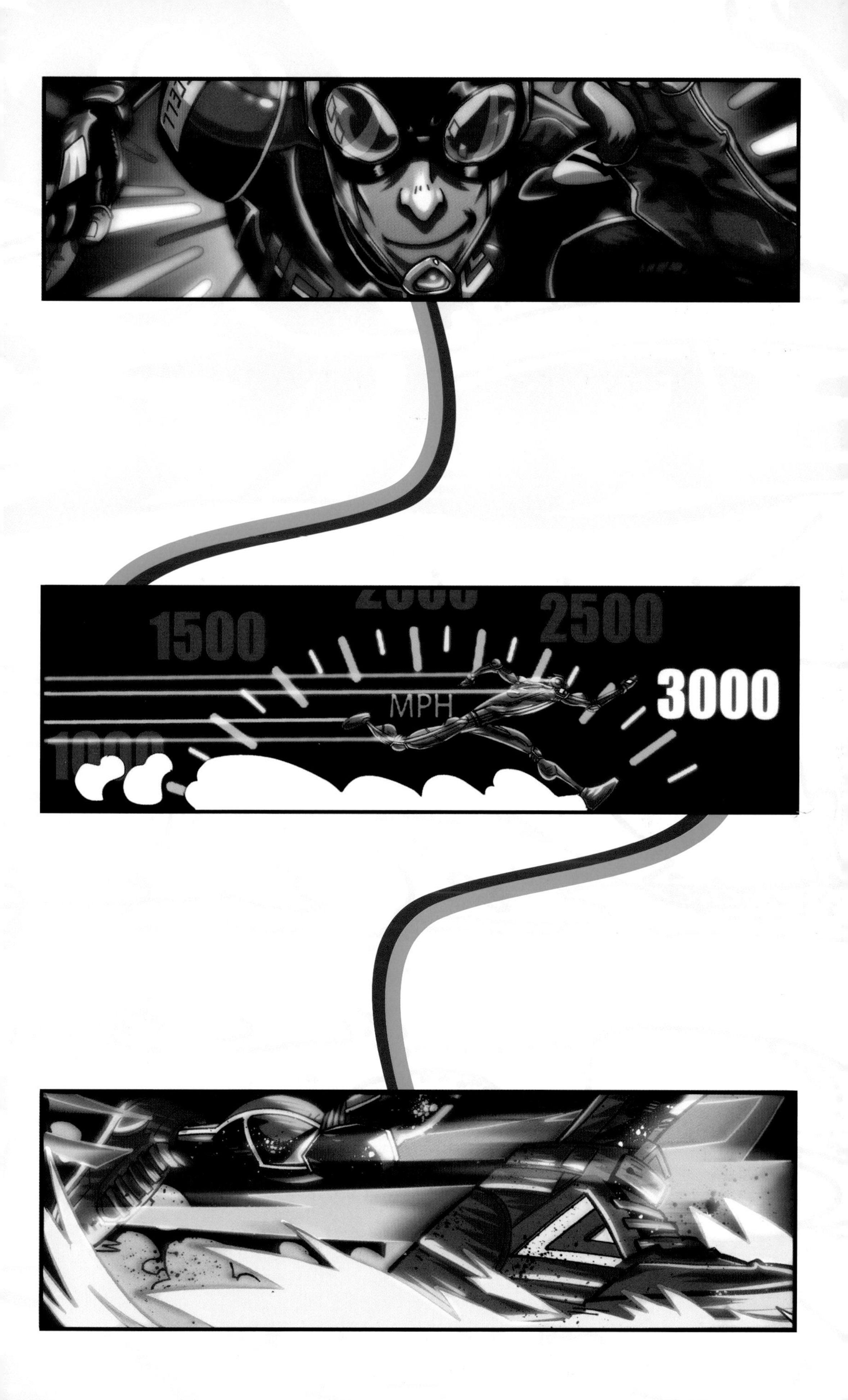
1500
2500
MPH
3000

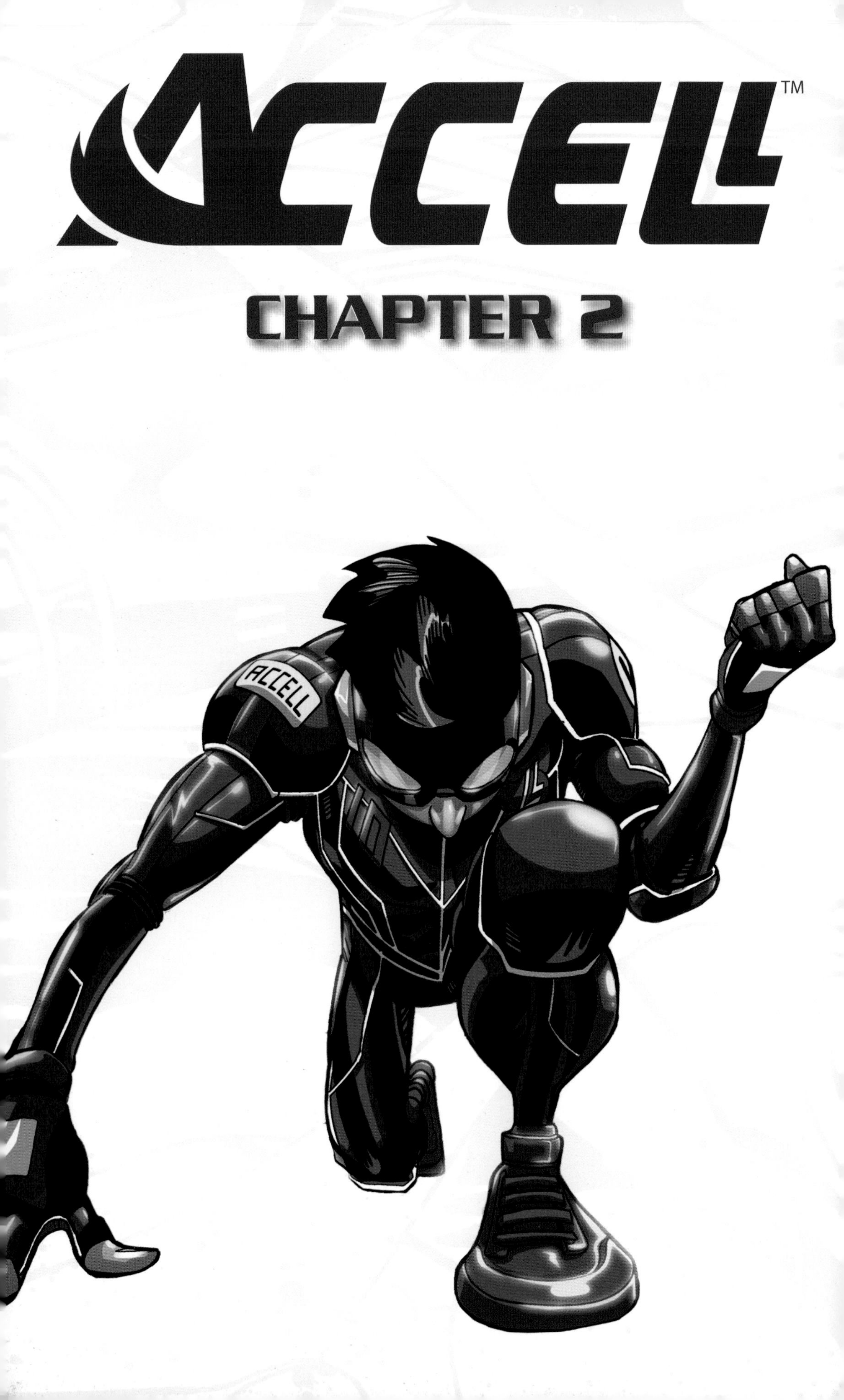
ACCEL™
CHAPTER 2
ACCELL

OKAY, I'LL ADMIT IT. SOMETIMES I DON'T KNOW WHAT THE HELL I'M DOING.
I MIGHT'VE WON OVER SOME WALKING ARSENAL THAT JACKED ME ON WILSHIRE BLVD, BUT I STILL ENDED UP BACK IN CEDARS FOR THE NIGHT...
...EVEN AS I HEALED MYSELF, I HAD A FEW MINOR EPIPHANIES.
I KINDA JUMPED INTO THIS WHOLE HERO THING. DIDN'T THINK MUCH ABOUT IT, AT FIRST. JUST THOUGHT IT WAS NINJA AS HELL.
NOW I'M EXPERIENCING A MAJOR RETHINK.

FIGURED I SHOULD FINALLY TEST MY LIMITS.
REALLY SEE WHAT I CAN DO WHEN I PUSH THESE NEW ABILITIES.
I'VE GOTTA SAY, IT WAS A PRETTY CONVENIENT EXCUSE, TOO...
...SO, I DON'T KNOW HOW LONG I'LL BE GONE.
IF YOU DON'T WANNA WAIT FOR ME, I TOTALLY GET IT.
CENTURY MALL
WHAT'RE YOU TALKING ABOUT, DANNY?! OF COURSE I'LL WAIT FOR YOU! THAT'S WHAT LOVE IS ALL ABOUT...!
WOW. THAT'S... REALLY SWEET OF YOU, BOMBONCITA...
I SUPPOSE I'M ABOUT AS GOOD AT THIS RELATIONSHIP STUFF AS I AM AT THIS SUPERHERO STUFF...
...WHICH IS NOT VERY WELL.
ARE YOU KIDDING?! WHEN I SAW YOU ON THE NEWS LAST NIGHT...AND THEY SAID YOU MIGHT BE DEAD...
...WELL, IF I DIDN'T KNOW BEFORE...NOW I'M SURE THIS IS MEANT TO BE!
SO, YEAH, I'LL WAIT FOR YOU. AS LONG AS IT TAKES.

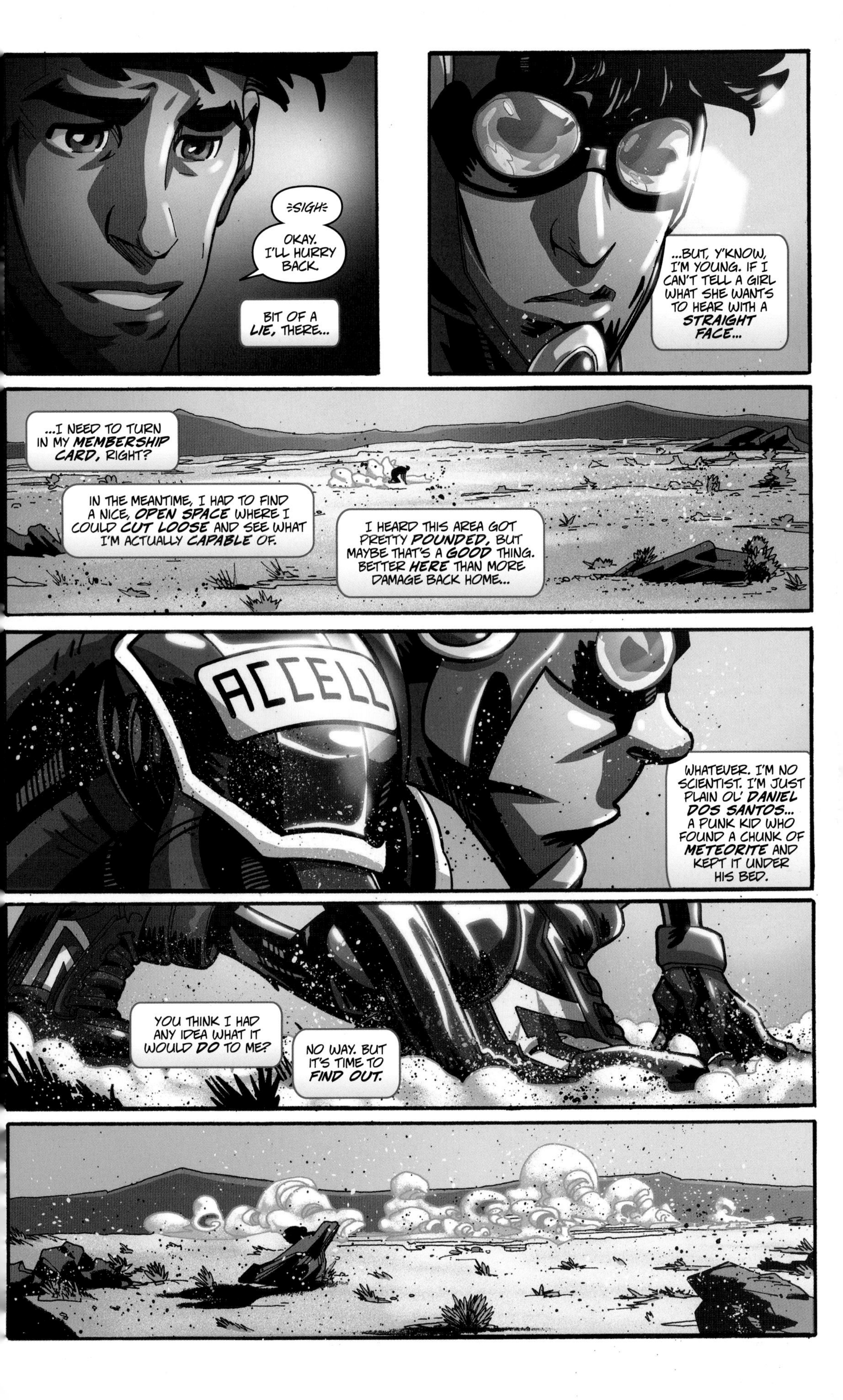

SIGH
OKAY. I'LL HURRY BACK.
BIT OF A LIE, THERE...
...BUT, Y'KNOW, I'M YOUNG. IF I CAN'T TELL A GIRL WHAT SHE WANTS TO HEAR WITH A STRAIGHT FACE...
...I NEED TO TURN IN MY MEMBERSHIP CARD, RIGHT?
IN THE MEANTIME, I HAD TO FIND A NICE, OPEN SPACE WHERE I COULD CUT LOOSE AND SEE WHAT I'M ACTUALLY CAPABLE OF.
I HEARD THIS AREA GOT PRETTY POUNDED, BUT MAYBE THAT'S A GOOD THING. BETTER HERE THAN MORE DAMAGE BACK HOME...
ACELL
WHATEVER. I'M NO SCIENTIST. I'M JUST PLAIN OL' DANIEL DOS SANTOS... A PUNK KID WHO FOUND A CHUNK OF METEORITE AND KEPT IT UNDER HIS BED.
YOU THINK I HAD ANY IDEA WHAT IT WOULD DO TO ME?
NO WAY. BUT IT'S TIME TO FIND OUT.

I CAN FEEL MY BODY MOVING. I CAN HEAR MY HEART BEATING. A SPLIT-SECOND LATER, IT'S THE ONLY THING I CAN HEAR.
ONE THING I KNEW RIGHT AWAY...IT WASN'T JUST THAT I WAS RUNNING FAST.
SOMETHING WAS HAPPENING TO THE WORLD IMMEDIATELY SURROUNDING ME.
IT FEELS LIKE I'M CUTTING A PATH THROUGH REALITY... BUT A REALITY THAT'S COME TO A COMPLETE STOP.
IS THAT POSSIBLE--?!

NO WIND RESISTANCE. NO REAL SENSE OF GRAVITY.
ALMOST LIKE BEING UNDERWATER.
FEELS KINDA COOL.
AFTER ALL, WHEN I'M NOT GETTING SMACKED AROUND OR SLAMMING INTO THINGS...WHY WOULDN'T THIS BE THE COOLEST THING EVER?!
1500
2000
3000
1000
IT'S EVEN COOLER THAN I THOUGHT IT WAS! I'M THE FASTEST THING ON TWO FEET!

THEN THINGS START TO GET WEIRD...
...ALL OF A SUDDEN, I DON'T KNOW WHAT'S REAL--
--AND WHAT ISN'T.
I THINK I SHOULD MAYBE SLOW DOWN...
BUT I CAN'T.
I DON'T WANT TO.

I'M FEELING SOMETHING... DEEP DOWN...
...A SENSE OF WHAT I'M DOING AS I MOVE THIS FAST...
...I'M NOT JUST RUNNING FAST...
...I'M AFFECTING THE ACTUAL PHYSICS OF REALITY...
...ON A PURELY PERCEPTIVE LEVEL, IT MIGHT BE TRANSLATING AS SUPER SPEED.
BUT IT'S SOMETHING ELSE. SOMETHING... DIFFERENT.
AND THEN... THINGS REALLY GET SCREWY.

I HAVE NO IDEA WHAT IT IS...OR WHAT IT'S DOING HERE...
...BUT IT MAKES A SOUND. THE ONLY SOUND I CAN HEAR. LIKE THE SPLITTING OF AN ATOM OR SOMETHING. WHATEVER IT IS--
--IT'S ENOUGH TO RUIN MY DAY.
TRUST ME. IT'S JUST AS PAINFUL AS IT LOOKS.

SOME OUTFIT T'BE SPORTIN' OUT ON THE BADLANDS...
...THINK MAYBE WE GOT ROOM FOR ONE MORE.
WHEN I FINALLY COME TO, I'M ACROSS A CAMPFIRE FROM SOME WEIRD OLD MAN. AS SOON AS I STOP DROOLING... HE STARTS TALKING...
...Y'KNOW, I'VE BEEN COMIN' OUT HERE FOR YEARS. IT'S A GOOD PLACE TO GET MY HEAD TOGETHER.
I IMAGINE THAT'S WHAT YOU'RE TRYIN' TO DO, EH, KID...?
I-I GUESS SO.
JUST ONE OF THOSE THINGS. I... HAD TO GET OUT OF L.A. FOR AWHILE, Y'KNOW?

I HEAR YOU. I WAS LIVING ON THE RESERVATION NEAR MIAMI, OKLAHOMA FOR YEARS. YEAH, THAT'S ITS NAME.
BUT EVEN THAT WASN'T WIDE OPEN ENOUGH FOR ME.
BESIDES... IT GOT HIT PRETTY HARD BY THE SKY FIRE...
SO YOU'RE A...
FORMER MEMBER OF THE SENECA NATION OF INDIANS. THE SENECA-CAYUGA TRIBE, TO BE SPECIFIC.
I ACKNOWLEDGE MY BLOOD, BUT I WAS NEVER MUCH OF A JOINER.
THEY CALLED ME LITTLE WING.
BUT YOU CAN CALL ME JESSE.
I CAME OUT HERE TO FIND THE TRUTH. I'VE BEEN HAVING RECURRING DREAMS...
UH-OH. I ALWAYS GET NERVOUS WHEN OLD PEOPLE START USING WORDS LIKE "TRUTH" AND "DREAMS"...
I DOUBT YOU'VE EVER HEARD OF THE LEGEND OF THE DAGWANOENYENT. NOT MANY HAVE.
A DEMON WHIRLWIND. DANGEROUS AND UNKILLABLE.

IT LIVES IN THE SKY ABOVE US...IT HOVERS THERE, WAITING TO STRIKE AT ANY MOMENT...
...THE THING IS, IF YOU CAN GET AHOLD OF OL' DAG...SPECIFICALLY, IF YOU CAN SNATCH THREE HAIRS FROM ITS DEMON HEAD...
...YOU CAN WORK MIRACLES.
GETTING TIRED...
WAIT.
WHAT IS THIS...SOME KIND OF NATIVE AMERICAN FOLKLORE...?
ONE MAN'S FOLKLORE IS ANOTHER MAN'S FACT, SON...
...AND SOME THINGS, WE'RE NOT MEANT TO FULLY UNDERSTAND. THIS MIGHT BE ONE OF 'EM.
SOMETIMES, IT JUST COMES DOWN TO WHAT YOU'RE WILLING TO BELIEVE.
RIGHT. I HAVE NO IDEA WHY HE JUST LAID ALL THAT ON ME...

...BUT, FOR NOW, I'M JUST GRATEFUL I CAN GET A LITTLE MORE SHUT-EYE. I NEED IT.
ACCELL
FOR THE RECORD, THIS IS NOT THE WAY YOU WANNA BE WOKEN UP...!
IS THIS WHAT THE OLD MAN WAS TALKING ABOUT?
I THINK I'M STARTING TO MISS JUST BEING SHOT AT...!

EVER HAVE ONE OF THOSE DAYS WHERE THINGS START MOVING TOO FAST...?
YOU'RE STILL TRYING TO PROCESS OLD INFORMATION...
CELL
"DEMON WHIRLWIND." I SHOULD'VE PAID CLOSER ATTENTION TO THE OLD MAN'S BEDTIME STORY...
...'CAUSE I THINK THAT'S EXACTLY WHAT I'M UP AGAINST!

IT CAME OUT OF NOWHERE. I CAN'T TELL IF IT'S PISSED OFF AT ME OR NOT.
BUT I REALLY DON'T WANNA FIND OUT.
WHATEVER IT IS--
--IT'S FAST.

THAT...WAS PAINFUL...
ACCELL
...UUUHHH...
NEED TO GET IT TOGETHER QUICK...
...WHAT ELSE DID THE OLD MAN SAY ABOUT IT?
"IT LIVES IN THE SKY ABOVE US...IT HOVERS THERE, WAITING TO STRIKE AT ANY MOMENT..."
THE SKY ABOVE US, HUH?
WELL, THAT DOESN'T EXPLAIN THE EARTHQUAKE I'M FEELING...

IF IT IS WHAT HE SAID IT IS...
WHAT'S HAPPENING? WHERE IS IT--
OH DAMN...!

ACCEL
SO I CAME OUT TO THE DESERT TO TEST MY LIMITS...TO SEE WHAT KIND OF SPEED I WAS ACTUALLY CAPABLE OF...
I FIGURE, IF I'M GOING TO DO THIS FOR REAL...I NEED TO KNOW WHAT I CAN AND CAN'T DO, RIGHT...?
ACCELL
I THOUGHT I WAS MOVING FAST BEFORE...
...GUESS I DIDN'T HAVE THE PROPER MOTIVATION.
THIS IS THAT SAME FEELING...LIKE I HAD EARLIER TODAY, RUNNING THE FLATS...
...JUST LIKE BEFORE... SOMETHING'S HAPPENING...
...TO REALITY ITSELF...!

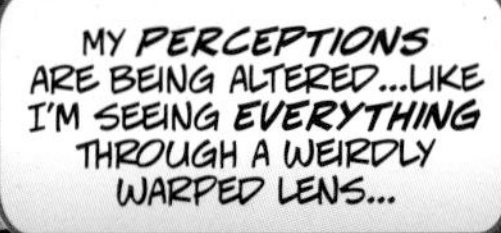
MY PERCEPTIONS ARE BEING ALTERED...LIKE I'M SEEING EVERYTHING THROUGH A WEIRDLY WARPED LENS...
...BUT IT'S SOMETHING MORE THAN JUST MY BRAIN BEING AFFECTED BY MY RATE OF SPEED...
...TRYING TO PROCESS WHAT I'M FEELING...SOMETIMES IN THE ONLY WAY MY BRAIN CAN HANDLE..
...AM I IMAGINING SOMETHING THAT DOESN'T EXIST? OR IS MOVING AT THIS SPEED OPENING SOME SORT OF DOORWAY TO SOMETHING YOU COULDN'T GET TO OTHERWISE...?
TO SOMETHING ELSE...?

...BUT I'M FEELING SOMETHING OUT THERE...SOMETHING BEYOND THE WORLD THAT I'VE ALWAYS KNOWN...
...SOME KIND OF PUNK ROCK STRING THEORY PULLING AT MY INSIDES...

I FORGET ABOUT THIS THING CHASING ME...
I'M MORE INTERESTED IN WHAT'S IN FRONT OF ME...TEASING ME...
ACCELL
...CALLING OUT TO ME...
...AND SUDDENLY... I'M ACTUALLY SEEING IT...
ACCELL
...I HAVE NO IDEA WHAT IT IS...
...BUT I CAN JUST...REACH IT...

...OR NOT.

I DON'T EVEN KNOW WHAT I'M SEEING HERE...I CAN'T TELL WHAT'S IN FRONT OF ME OR BEHIND ME...
...MY MIND TURNS INSIDE-OUT...

...AND ALL I CAN DO IS ACT ON INSTINCT.
MY BRAIN IS TRYING TO CONVINCE ME THAT I'VE STOPPED...BUT SOMETHING ELSE INSIDE ME IS STILL MOVING...
...THIS DOESN'T MAKE SENSE OTHERWISE.
WHAT IS THIS...?
WAIT.
SOMETHING BEHIND ME--

--UH OH...!

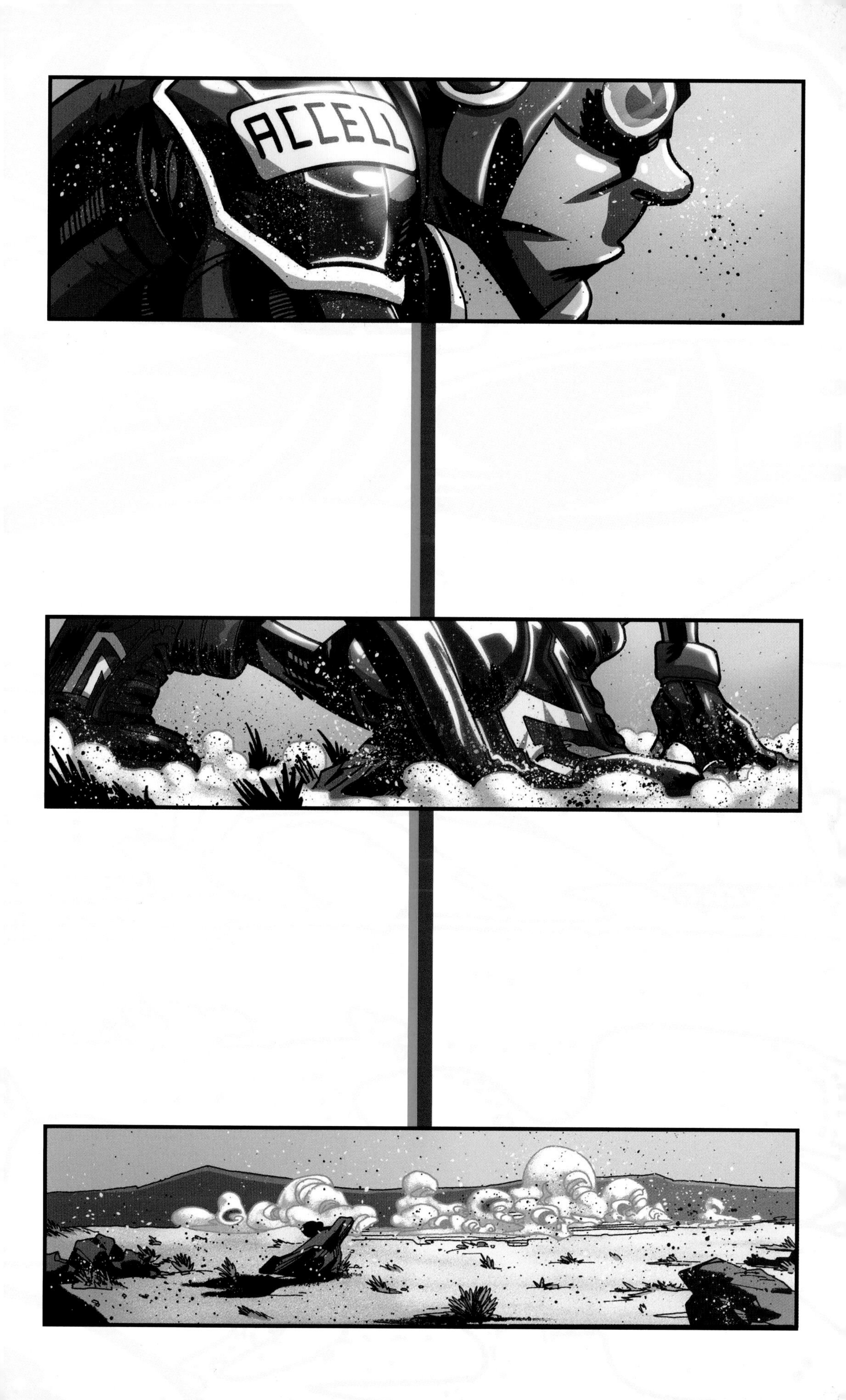
ACCELL

CHAPTER 3

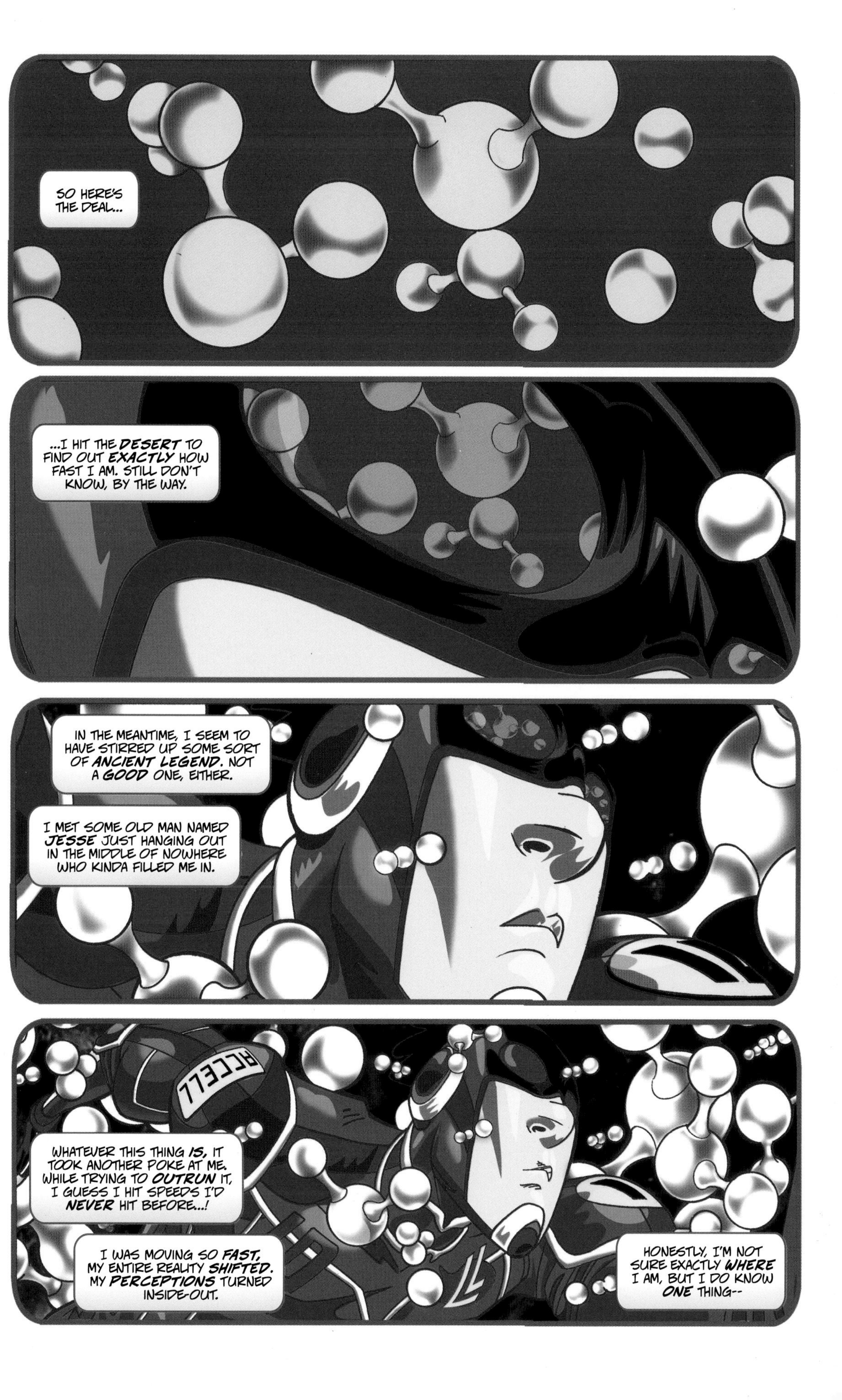
SO HERE'S THE DEAL...
...I HIT THE DESERT TO FIND OUT EXACTLY HOW FAST I AM. STILL DON'T KNOW, BY THE WAY.
IN THE MEANTIME, I SEEM TO HAVE STIRRED UP SOME SORT OF ANCIENT LEGEND. NOT A GOOD ONE, EITHER.
I MET SOME OLD MAN NAMED JESSE JUST HANGING OUT IN THE MIDDLE OF NOWHERE WHO KINDA FILLED ME IN.
ACCELL
WHATEVER THIS THING IS, IT TOOK ANOTHER POKE AT ME. WHILE TRYING TO OUTRUN IT, I GUESS I HIT SPEEDS I'D NEVER HIT BEFORE...!
I WAS MOVING SO FAST, MY ENTIRE REALITY SHIFTED. MY PERCEPTIONS TURNED INSIDE-OUT.
HONESTLY, I'M NOT SURE EXACTLY WHERE I AM, BUT I DO KNOW ONE THING--

--THE DAMN THING
FOLLOWED ME IN.

ACCELL

IT'S LIKE...WE'RE VIBRATING AT A DIFFERENT WAVELENGTH THAN "NORMAL" REALITY...
AND THE LAST THING I WANT IS TO GET KILLED UP IN HERE!
WAIT A SEC. MAYBE THERE'S A WAY TO DEAL WITH THIS MONSTER, AT LEAST...
SOMETHING THE OLD MAN SAID...
...THE THING IS, IF YOU CAN GET AHOLD OF OL' DAG... SPECIFICALLY, IF YOU CAN SNATCH THREE HAIRS FROM ITS DEMON HEAD...
...YOU CAN WORK MIRACLES.
HOPE HE WAS RIGHT--

--CAUSE I COULD USE A MIRACLE ABOUT NOW!
RIGHT. WHATEVER THIS STUFF IS, I'VE GOT A GOOD GRIP ON IT.
NOW IT'S TIME TO PUT ON THE BRAKES--

--IF HITTING A CERTAIN SPEED PUT ME IN THIS PLACE, MAYBE SLOWING DOWN WILL GET ME OUT OF IT!
THIS IS WHERE THE "MIRACLE" PART SHOULD KICK IN.
PLEASE LET THIS WORK--

ACCELL
WOW. CHECK ME OUT--
--PULSE IS RACING. BRAIN'S POUNDING IN MY SKULL. BUT I MADE IT **BACK!**

ACCELL
LOOKS LIKE IT'S STILL PISSED OFF, THOUGH...
HANG ON--
--MAYBE I CAN STILL TAKE A RIDE ON THE MIRACLE TRAIN.
THAT IS, IF THIS TRAIN DOESN'T RUN ME DOWN FIRST...!

TOO CLOSE FOR COMFORT--
--AND IT JUST OCCURRED TO ME...IF WE'RE REALLY BACK IN THE REALITY I KNOW AND LOVE...
...WHAT'S THE OLD MAN UP TO...?!
OVER HERE, KID!
THAT'S MY NIGHTMARE YOU'RE WRESTLIN' WITH!
THAT'S OL' DAG!

IF THIS IS THAT DAG-WHATEVER HE WAS TELLING ME ABOUT, MAYBE HE KNOWS WHAT TO DO --
--BETTER THAN I DO, THAT'S FOR SURE...!
ACCE
...GOTTA BE HERE...!
...KNOW DAMN WELL I BROUGHT IT WITH ME...!
AND THERE YOU ARE, KID...!
WAIT! WE CAN BURN IT UP!
FIRE AND AIR--
YYYNNNGG--!
YOU GOTTA LEAD HIM BACK T'ME!
ONLY ONE THING TO DO--!

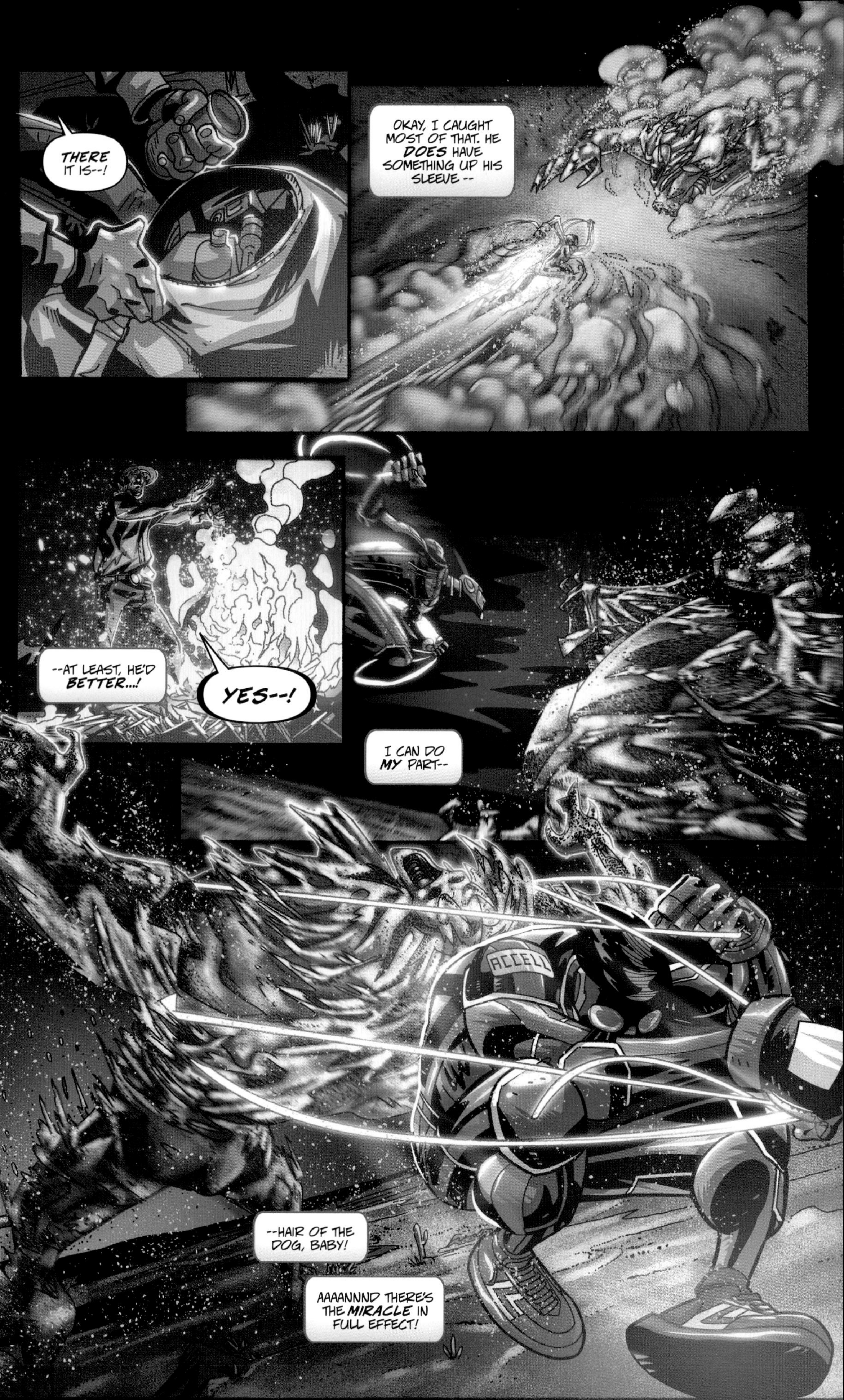
THERE IT IS--!
OKAY, I CAUGHT MOST OF THAT. HE DOES HAVE SOMETHING UP HIS SLEEVE --
--AT LEAST, HE'D BETTER...!
YES--!
I CAN DO MY PART--
ACCEL
--HAIR OF THE DOG, BABY!
AAAANNND THERE'S THE MIRACLE IN FULL EFFECT!

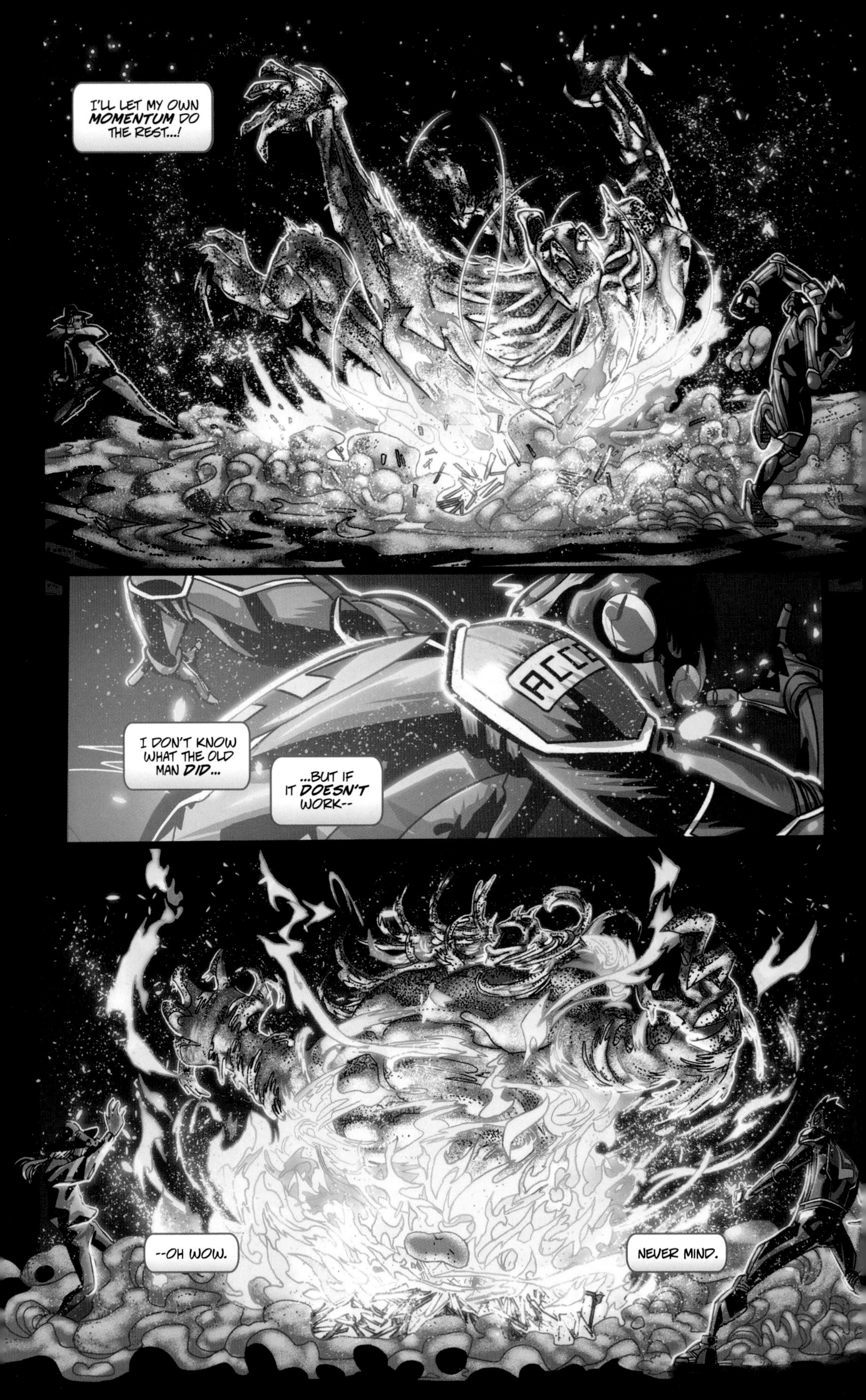
I'LL LET MY OWN MOMENTUM DO THE REST...!
I DON'T KNOW WHAT THE OLD MAN DID...
...BUT IF IT DOESN'T WORK--
--OH WOW.
NEVER MIND.

WHOA...!
THAT WORKED, DIDN'T IT...?
PANT!
PANT!
PANT!
Y-YES IT DID...
MAN, YOU WEREN'T KIDDING WITH YOUR LITTLE BEDTIME STORY...
...BUT WHAT WAS THAT THING?
EXACTLY WHAT I TOLD YOU IT WAS--
--DAGWANOENYENT. THE DEMON WHIRLWIND.
WHEW
KICKS UP ONE HELLUVA RUCKUS, DON'T IT...?
YOU HAVE NO IDEA.
HOLD ON NOW...YOU ALSO SAID HE WAS "UNKILLABLE". SO WHAT JUST HAPPENED...?
RETURNING TO THE SKY...ISN'T THE SAME DEATH... THAT WE KNOW OF...
IT'S... SOMETHING ELSE...
HUH...
H-HEY...YOU OKAY...?
HNNGGK--!
GYAK!
N-N-NNNNN...

JESSE--!
WHAT'S GOING ON?!
AHHH...
HEY--!
MUH...
...MUH HEART...!
NNG!
OH DAMN.
I'LL... GET YOU TO A HOSPITAL...!
PROBLEM: I DON'T KNOW ANY HOSPITALS TO GO TO AROUND HERE! I BARELY KNOW WHERE I AM!
ONLY THING I CAN DO IS GET HIM BACK TO L.A.--
--AND I'LL BET I'VE PROBABLY GOT ABOUT ONE HEARTBEAT LEFT TO DO IT!

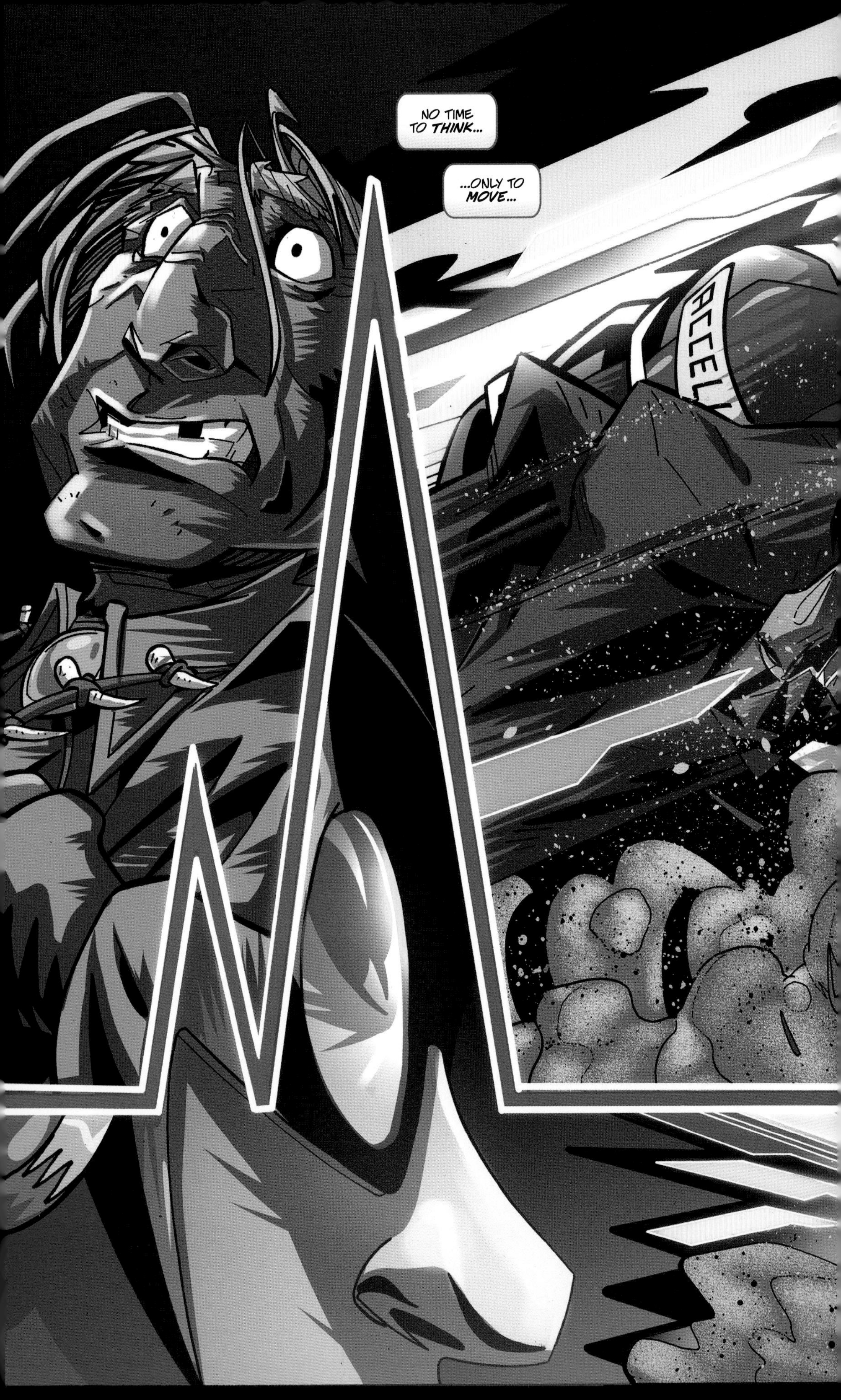
NO TIME TO *THINK*...
...ONLY TO *MOVE*...

...IN THE BRIEF MOMENT BETWEEN HEARTBEATS...
...I JUST HOPE THAT I DON'T SLIP BACK INTO THAT PLACE... WHATEVER IT WAS...

...BUT I'M TOO FOCUSED...
...I'M NOT STRAYING OFF THE PATH THIS TIME...THE ONE THAT LEADS SOMEWHERE...
...A MAN'S LIFE IS LITERALLY IN MY HANDS...

...IS THIS WHAT BEING A SUPERHERO IS ALL *ABOUT?*

GAH--!
WE MADE IT.
NEED A DOCTOR OVER HERE--!
N-NO...
TOO LATE...FOR THAT...
...SHOULDN'T HAVE...BROUGHT ME HERE...
WHU... WHAT'RE YOU TALKIN' ABOUT?!
C'MON...LET THESE GUYS DO THEIR THING...
THE SKY...IT'S CALLING TO ME NOW, TOO...
...NO MESSIN' WITH THAT...
...EVERYTHING WE ARE...IS A PART OF...SOMETHING BIGGER...
WEIRD.
IT DIDN'T FEEL LIKE A MAN DIED IN MY ARMS...
...FELT MORE LIKE I'D SENT HIM ON HIS WAY.

I DO WHAT I CAN TO SHAKE IT OFF...
...TRY TO DO "NORMAL" STUFF.
GO, BOY!
YOU'RE GETTING SOME SERIOUS AIR, DANNY!
MY OWN HOSPITAL STAY WAS BRIEF. FOR ONCE, I HADN'T PUT MY BODY THROUGH HELL...
LOOKING GOOD OUT THERE.
YOU FEEL ANY BETTER? FEEL LIKE TELLING ME WHAT HAPPENED TO YOU YESTERDAY...?
NOT JUST YET.

HEY, MONICA... I APPRECIATE YOU COMING OUT HERE TO HANG AN' EVERYTHING. I'M JUST...
IT'S OKAY. I JUST WANT YOU TO KNOW THAT I'M ABSOLUTELY, ONE HUNDRED PERCENT--
YO YO YO...
...IS THIS THE NEW HOTNESS I SEE BEFORE ME?
LEAVE IT TO BUZZ TO BAIL ME OUT OF AN AWKWARD RELATIONSHIP MOMENT...
...NOT THAT THIS KID EVER KNOWS WHAT HE'S DOING.
DANNY, MY BRUTHA--
--WHUDDUP?
'SUP, FAM... NOT TOO MUCH.
YOU HEAR ABOUT THE COPS DOIN' A SWEEP THROUGH HERE LAST WEEK? I HEARD THEY WERE LOOKIN' FOR DRUGS...
...I MEAN, Y'DIG THAT?
EWW. IS THAT SUPPOSED TO BE SOME KIND OF A JOKE, BUZZ?
SO DID YOU GET POPPED?
C'MON, GIRL. YOU KNOW ME...
...I'M A GANGSTA DAT NEVER GETS PINCHED.
I SEE HER, SIR. SHE'S RIGHT ACROSS THE STREET FROM WHERE I'M PARKED--

--AND SHE'S WITH HIM, AS PREDICTED.
I MUST SAY, SIR, I DON'T FEEL ENTIRELY COMFORTABLE ENACTING THIS KIND OF SURVEILLANCE ON YOUR DAUGHTER...
LET ME TELL YOU SOMETHING, ARTHUR...
...I DON'T GIVE A DAMN WHAT YOU FEEL "COMFORTABLE" WITH RIGHT NOW.
I SIGN YOUR PAYCHECK. IF I TELL YOU TO BEND OVER AND SMILE ABOUT IT, THAT'S WHAT YOU DO.
YOU HEAR ME?
=GULP!=
I DO INDEED.
NOW I TOLD YOU...I DON'T WANT MY LITTLE MONICA TO HAVE ANYTHING TO DO WITH DOS SANTOS!
BUT SHE'S A VERY WILLFUL GIRL. JUST LIKE HER MOTHER WAS.
FOR NOW, YOU'RE GOING TO KEEP VERY CLOSE TABS ON HER WHILE I CONTEMPLATE MY NEXT MOVE...!
...SO, YEAH, HE MADE LIKE A PHANTOM. HAVEN'T SEEN HIM SINCE.
SOUNDS LIKE IT ALL WORKED OUT, THEN...FOR YOU, AT LEAST.
DO YOU MIND...?!
I LET THEM CHATTER... AND HOPE THAT IT LETS ME AT LEAST PRETEND THAT EVERYTHING'S COOL.

PERSONALLY, I THINK YOU COULD DO A LOT BETTER THAN THOSE LOSERS, BUZZ...
...YOU DON'T SEE DANNY HANGING AROUND THEIR STUPID CARD GAMES, DO YOU?
IT'S NOT REALLY WORKING, THOUGH. THEIR VOICES FADE INTO THE BACKGROUND AND I'M SOMEWHERE ELSE...
...SOMEWHERE THAT STILL CALLS OUT TO ME...
...SOMEWHERE THAT I'M NOT SURE IF I BELONG TO OR NOT...
...DID JESSE KNOW MORE THAN HE EVER TOLD ME...?
...EVERYTHING WE ARE...IS A PART OF...SOMETHING BIGGER...
IT'S LIKE I'VE CROSSED SOME INVISIBLE LINE IN THE SAND...AND I DON'T KNOW IF I CAN GET BACK OVER TO WHERE I WAS...WHERE I'M SUPPOSED TO BE...
MAYBE EVEN WORSE THAN THAT... AFTER EVERYTHING I'VE SEEN...
...I'M NOT SO SURE THAT I WANT TO.

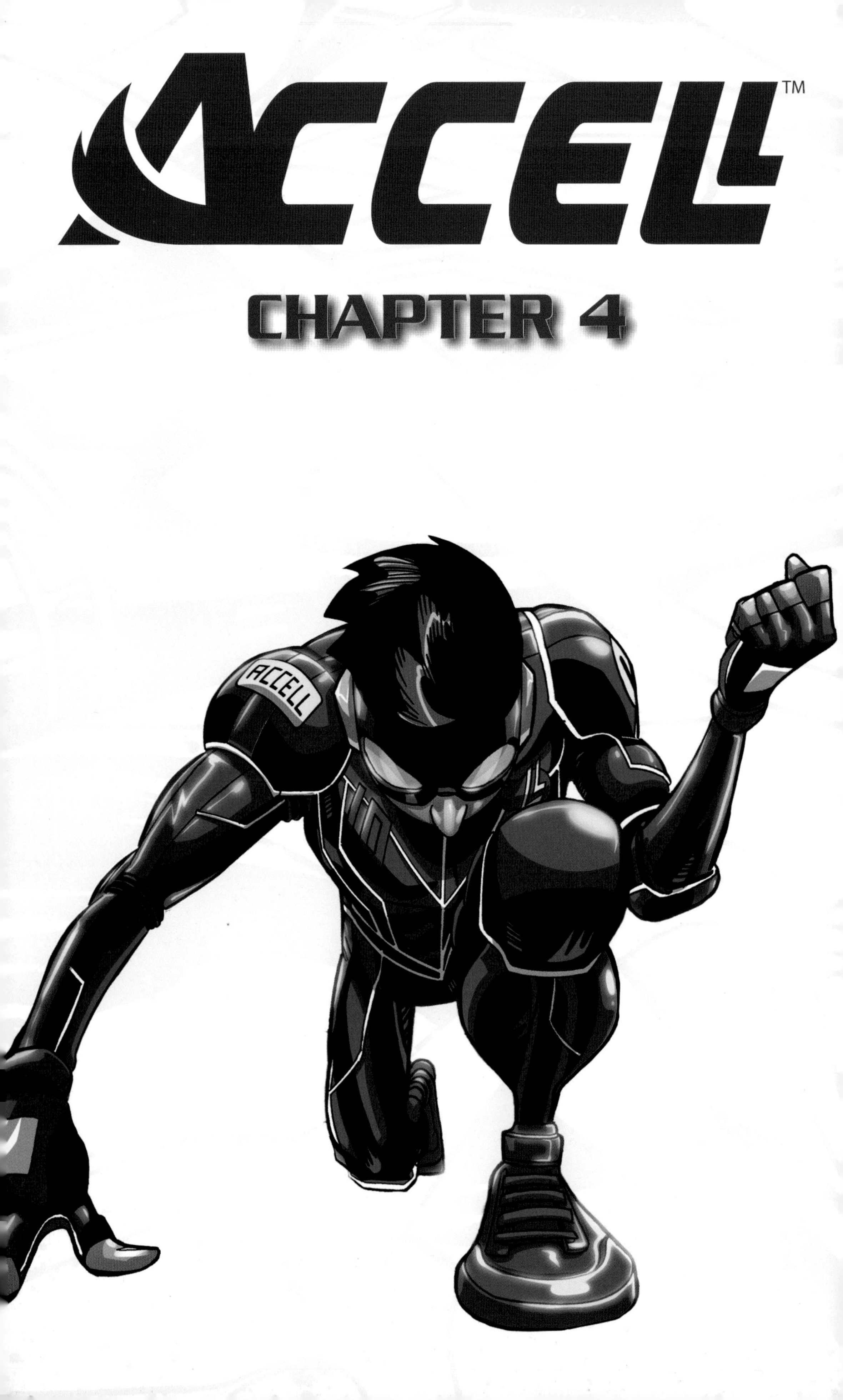
ACCEL™
CHAPTER 4
ACCELL

SOMETIMES I WONDER HOW I GOT HERE...
...SO I DON'T KNOW WHAT HE WAS THINKING! HE JUST KEPT GOING WITH IT...!
GOT A HIGH TOLERANCE, THAT ONE...
--SPENT SOME TIME IN THE COUNTY COOLER, Y'KNOW. TRAFFIC TICKETS GONE TO WARRANT...
...DOCKED ME A DAY'S PAY JUST 'CAUSE I WAS THREE HOURS LATE. I SHOULDA BUSTED HIS HEAD OPEN...
ANYONE KNOW WHERE I CAN GET A HOLD OF A SET OF LUG WRENCHES?
THE RED STATE AFFAIR
THEY JUST GO ON AND ON AROUND ME. I'M HERE...BUT I'M NOT REALLY HERE...

IT'S ALMOST LIKE I'M SLEEPWALKING THROUGH ALL THE NORMAL STUFF I USED TO DO...
...I THOUGHT SHE LOOKED HEAVY, I DUNNO.
MAYBE IT WAS JUST WATER RETENTION OR SOMETHING...
Y-YEAH... MAYBE...
IT'S HARD TO PRETEND I'M ACTUALLY LISTENING TO WHATEVER NONSENSE MONICA IS SAYING..
...IT'S DIFFICULT ENOUGH JUST TO WALK AT A NORMAL PACE.
ACCEL
I'VE GOTTEN USED TO THINGS MOVING A LOT FASTER.
...I JUST LOVE THAT SONG SO MUCH, Y'KNOW?
DON'T YOU HAVE SOMETHING LIKE THAT...THAT JUST, I DUNNO, TAKES YOU SOMEPLACE...?
UMMM... NOTHING THAT I CAN THINK OF RIGHT NOW...

HEY, DANNY...
...I DON'T KNOW ABOUT YOU, BUT I THINK THINGS BETWEEN US ARE GOING GREAT.
YEAH...?
YEAH.
I DON'T CARE WHAT MY FATHER SAYS...
THIS IS NOT GOOD...
... I SHOULDN'T BE DOING THIS...
... SPYING ON THE BOSS' DAUGHTER...
I'M JUST A HAYES COMPANY ACCOUNTANT...
...I'M NOT A CHAPERONE...
MONICA'S A SWEET GIRL, NO DOUBT ABOUT IT. SHE PROBABLY DESERVES A LOT BETTER THAN ME RIGHT NOW.

I JUST CAN'T HELP IT, THOUGH...
...I CAN'T IGNORE WHAT HAPPENED TO ME.
I KNOW IT MEANS SOMETHING...
...I JUST HAVEN'T FIGURED OUT WHAT YET.
I KNOW IT'S NOT FAIR TO HER. SHE'S REALLY TRYING.
GUESS THE LEAST I COULD DO IS RECIPROCATE...

...ALTHOUGH I AM CURIOUS WHAT SHE MEANT BY, "I DON'T CARE WHAT MY FATHER SAYS".
SO THIS IS WHERE YOU'VE BEEN HIDING OUT--
?!
--YOU REALLY THOUGHT I WOULDN'T FIND YOU?

WHEN GEORGE HAYES HIRES SOMEONE TO DO SOMETHING...I EXPECT NOTHING LESS THAN TOTAL SUCCESS.
IF I RECALL, I PAID YOU A HANDSOME FEE TO DEAL WITH THAT DOS SANTOS KID...
...AND WE BOTH KNOW HE'S STILL OUT THERE...HANGING AROUND WITH MY DAUGHTER.
YOU GOT BALLS ON YOU, HAYES...WALTZING IN HERE TO TELL ME WHAT'S UP...?!
YOU DON'T MESS WITH BARRAGE...
...UNLESS YOU'RE A FAN OF PAIN--
SAVE THE TOUGH GUY LINES. I'M NOT BUYING IT.
NOW-- WHERE'S MY MONEY?!
I'M HERE FOR MY REFUND--
--FOR SERVICES NOT RENDERED!

HUH...YOU'D THINK WITH ALL THIS WEAPONRY AT YOUR FINGERTIPS, YOU'D HAVE NO PROBLEM GETTING THE JOB DONE.
I'M SURE YOUR CHRISTMAS CARDS ARE DAMN IMPRESSIVE.
I KNOW YOU COULDN'T POSSIBLY AFFORD ALL THIS GEAR.
THAT'S...
...NONE OF YER BUSINESS...
SO WHO FRONTED YOU? AND WHO ARE YOU GIVING KICKBACKS TO SO I DON'T GET MY MONEY...?!
YOU DON'T THINK SO?! WELL, LET ME CLUE YOU IN ON SOMETHING--
--THIS IS MY BUSINESS! SO YOU WILL TELL ME OR YOU'RE GONNA KNOW SOME PAIN!

STILL TRYING TO ACT LIKE EVERYTHING IS "NORMAL"...
--WATCH OUT, BEHIND THE PILES!
I GOT HIM, I GOT HIM...KEEP YOUR DIAPER DRY, COSMO...
100 POINTS
4
3
RCAM-SIG DUO
0110/17
THESE ARE MY FRIENDS I'M PLAYING WITH. I'VE NEVER HUNG OUT WITH ANY OF THEM IN PERSON. BUT WE GET ON THE BOX AND WE SHOOT 'EM UP AND WE TALK SMACK AND IT'S NOT WEIRD AT ALL...
CAN WE GET THROUGH THIS LEVEL ALREADY?!
CALM DOWN, KEV!
YEAH, KEV... DON'T SWEAT IT...THERE'S ONLY TWO MORE DRONE SQUADRONS TO GO HERE...
...BY THE WAY, ANYONE SEE THE DEMO FOR ARCLIGHT VII? LOOKS INTENSE...
I HEARD THE BOSS BATTLES ARE WACK. AND THE CUT SCENES ARE BUGGY...
NEED SOME HELP OVER HERE, GUYS--!
DON'T LEAVE ME HANGING, PLEASE...!
I HATE TO HEAR YOU BEG, KEV...
YOU SURE YOU'RE OLD ENOUGH TO PLAY THIS GAME?
SHUT UP, TIG!
WE HAVE A GOOD TIME HARASSING KEVIN, THIS KID FROM SOMEWHERE IN MISSOURI, I THINK. HE'S LIKE, FIFTEEN, AND SOMEHOW ENDED UP IN OUR LITTLE ONLINE CADRE... NOW HE'S A PUNCHING BAG...

SOMETIMES THEY TALK ABOUT **PERSONAL** STUFF...I TRY TO **IGNORE** IT MOST OF THE TIME...
YOU KNOW I GOT **FINALS** NEXT WEEK? I SHOULD BE **STUDYING...**
YOU AFRAID YOUR MOMMY'S GONNA STOP SENDING YOU **MONEY,** JONESY? **HA!**
SORRY, GUYS...I GOTTA **BAIL** SOON. MY **BROTHER--**
OH, **COME ON!** YOU GONNA LET **THAT** JARHEAD TERRORIZE YOU FOR THE REST OF YOUR **LIFE?!**
I **DON'T,** OKAY?!
HE JUST... DOESN'T LIKE WHEN I'M HOGGING THE TV...
YEAH, RIGHT...
WAIT A SECOND. THIS IS STARTING TO SOUND A LITTLE **TOO** REAL...

DIDN'T HE BREAK YOUR **WRIST** THAT ONE TIME--
OH, DAMN...I THINK I HEAR HIS **CAR** PULLING UP...
YOU BETTER GET **OUT** OF THERE, YO...!

HOLD ON.
WHAT'S YOUR LAST NAME, KEV? WHERE DO YOU LIVE?
HIS LAST NAME'S **WALDECK.** LIVES IN WILDWOOD, I THINK...
HEY! WHAT'RE YOU TELLING **HIM** THAT FOR?!

YOUR MOM DOESN'T EVEN GIVE A DAMN, DOES SHE...?!
OH NO... HE JUST--
YOU LITTLE BASTARD! DIDN'T YOU LEARN NOTHIN' FROM THE LAST BEATING--?!
OH JEEZ... I CAN'T LISTEN TO THIS...
IS THAT HIS--
--BROTHER--
WILDWOOD, MISSOURI...
ACCEL
...HERE I COME.

--I'M HEARIN' IN THE BACKGROUND?
YUP. TIME TO LOG OFF, GUYS..
WHAT'D I TELL YOU--
--WHEN I'M HERE, YOU AIN'T GOT NO TV PRIVILEGES!
JIM! DON'T--
--I'M GETTING OFF! I'M GETTING OFF!
YOU'RE DAMN RIGHT YOU ARE!
AND I'M GONNA MAKE SURE YOU DON'T FORGET--

--TIME FOR ANOTHER PAINFUL LESSON, KID!
PLEASE-PLEASE--PLEASE! NO--
YOU GONNA START CRYIN' NOW?!
HUUHHNDT--!
WHEN ARE YOU GONNA BE A MAN, HUH?!
IF I GOTTA BEAT IT INTO YOU--
--THEN I WILL!
AUUGH--!
DROP THE KID, CHINGADO...

...OR I MAY HAVE TO DROP **YOU**.
THANK GOD FOR GOOGLE. THERE WERE **EIGHT** "WALDECK'S" IN WILDWOOD. THIS WAS MY **SIXTH** STOP. TOOK ME NINE SECONDS.
AS FAR AS **SMACK TALK** GOES... NOT TOO BAD, I GUESS.
WE'LL SEE HOW WELL IT **WORKS**...

WHAT IS THIS --HALLOWEEN?!
YOU THREATENING ME?! I'LL TAKE YOU DOWN, CLOWN!
UUHHH...?
YOU WILL, HUH?
GOTTA CATCH ME FIRST, BIG TIME.
OH, I WILL!
AND WHEN I DO, I'M GONNA TEAR YOU APART!
YOU AND YOUR FRUITY OUTFIT!
"FRUITY OUTFIT"? PUH-LEEZE...!
GUUHN--!
YOU'RE JUST LIVING UP TO ALL THE STEREOTYPES, AREN'T YOU?!
W-WAIT...

WELL, HELL... LET'S SEE WHAT WE CAN DO ABOUT THAT.
I COULD PROBABLY BEAT 'EM OUTTA YOU!
MAYBE NEXT TIME YOU FEEL LIKE POUNDING ON YOUR HERMANITO--YOU'LL REMEMBER WHAT THIS FEELS LIKE AND THINK TWICE!
UHHHH...
I MEAN, SOUNDS LIKE A PLAN TO ME--
NO! STOP!
PLEASE--
--DON'T HURT MY BROTHER!
SAY WHAT...?!
I DON'T GET IT... DON'T YOU WANNA SEE THIS SCUMBAG GET WHAT'S COMING TO HIM?!
P-PLEASE... WHOEVER YOU ARE...

...JUST LET HIM GO...
YOU GOTTA BE KIDDING ME...!
YOU THINK THIS PIECE OF GARBAGE DESERVES ONE OUNCE OF COMPASSION?! ARE YOU SERIOUS?
Y-YEAH... I MAY HATE HIM... BUT...
...HE'S STILL MY BROTHER.
FINE.
SORRY, KEV. I DON'T HAVE SIBLINGS.
HUUHHN...!
WELL, THERE IT IS...
...ANOTHER SWING AND A MISS IN THE HERO DEPARTMENT.
ACCELL

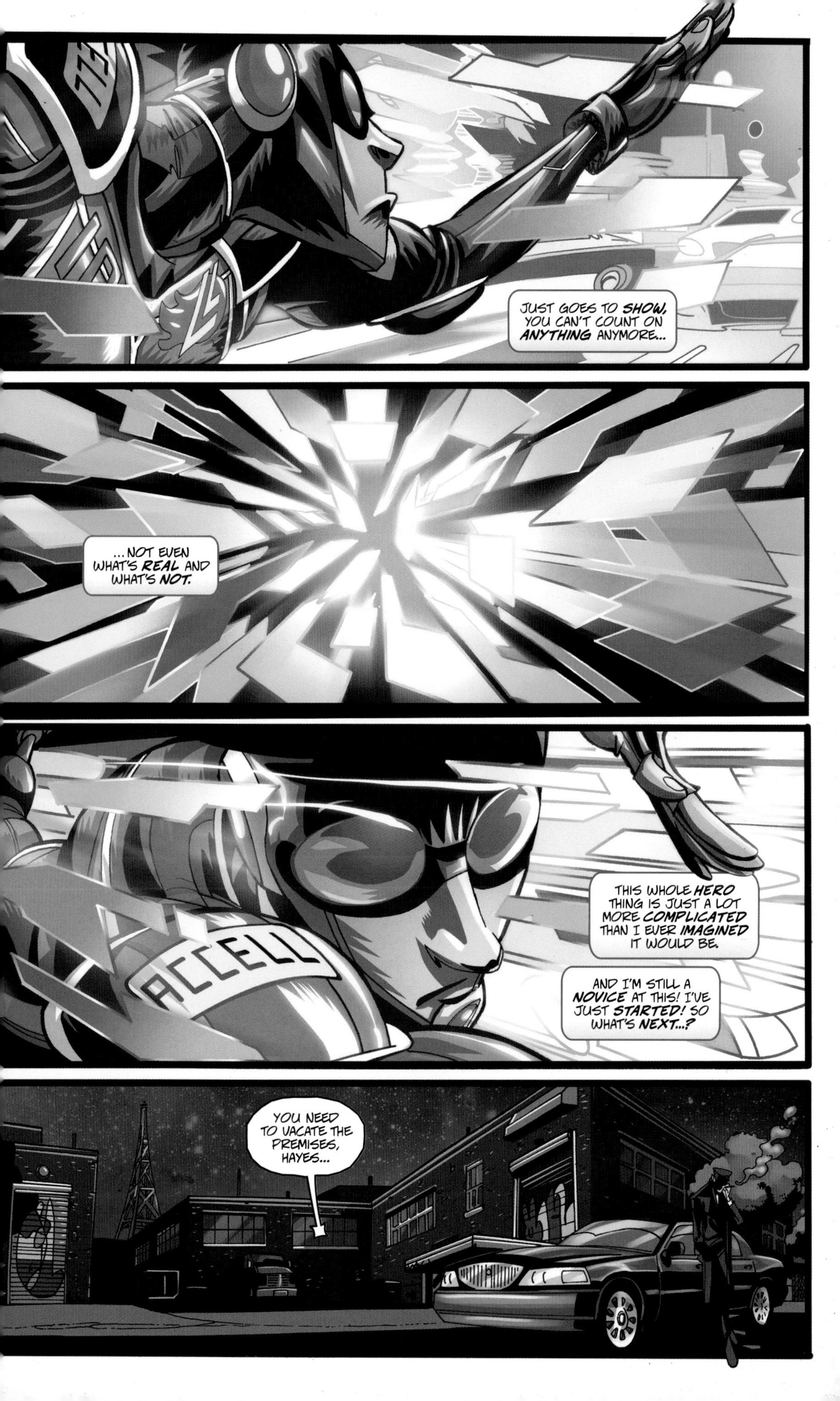
JUST GOES TO SHOW, YOU CAN'T COUNT ON ANYTHING ANYMORE...
...NOT EVEN WHAT'S REAL AND WHAT'S NOT.
ACCELL
THIS WHOLE HERO THING IS JUST A LOT MORE COMPLICATED THAN I EVER IMAGINED IT WOULD BE.
AND I'M STILL A NOVICE AT THIS! I'VE JUST STARTED! SO WHAT'S NEXT...?
YOU NEED TO VACATE THE PREMISES, HAYES...

...YOU AIN'T GOT WHAT IT TAKES TO PLAY AT THIS LEVEL.
GO BACK TO YER BOARDROOM AND YER STOCK OPTIONS...
...AND TRY NOT TO THINK OF YER DAUGHTER BANGIN' THAT SPEED FREAK.
THAT'S IT!
IT'S BAD ENOUGH YOU CAN'T ACTUALLY ACCOMPLISH WHAT I PAID YOU TO DO--
--NOW YOU'RE GIVING ME ATTITUDE?!
I SEE WHAT YOU'RE ABOUT NOW! SO FOR THE LAST TIME--
--WHO DO I TALK TO ABOUT GETTING MY MONEY BACK?!

UHHH... OKAY, OKAY... DAMN...
...MOST OF MY EARNINGS FROM THIS GIG...
...GO STRAIGHT TO GLAZZ.
"GLAZZ"?!
WHAT THE HELL IS A "GLAZZ"?!
I DON'T KNOW WHAT TO TELL YOU, MISTER GLAZZ...
...I COULDN'T MAKE MY NUT THIS MONTH.
A COUPLE OF MY ACCOUNTS WENT AWOL. SKIPPED TOWN, Y'KNOW? HOW CAN I COLLECT WHEN THEY'VE UP AND DISAPPEARED...?
TOUGH BREAK, MAURICE--
--REALLY TOUGH BREAK.
FOR YOU, I MEAN.

IT'S FUNNY, REALLY... YOU COMING TO ME ASKING FOR SOME MEASURE OF MERCY WHEN YOU CAN'T PAY UP ON WHAT YOU OWE ME...
YOU KNOW HOW I DEAL WITH SITUATIONS LIKE THIS...
CLEAN AND SIMPLE.
I DON'T HAVE TIME FOR DEAD WEIGHT IN MY CITY.
THAT'S WHO GLAZZ IS...
SO HE RUNS THE UNDERWORLD, IS THAT IT? ALL THE FREAKS ON THE STREET ANSWER TO HIM?
NOT A BAD BUSINESS TO BE IN, IS IT...?

MY HEAD'S STILL SPINNING...
...SEEMS LIKE EVERY TIME I TRY TO GET A HANDLE ON THIS THING, IT BLOWS UP IN MY FACE. AND HERE I THOUGHT HAVING SUPER-SPEED WOULD MAKE MY LIFE EASIER...!
I GUESS THERE'S NO SUCH THING AS A FREE RIDE...
...NOT WHEN YOU'RE PLAYING THIS GAME, ANYWAY.
HMMM...
...PRETTY DARK NIGHT IN THE CITY OF ANGELS.
PLENTY OF WEIRDNESS GOES DOWN WHEN THIS DARKNESS FALLS... BUT I REALLY BELIEVE...

...IT COULD STAND TO GET A LOT DARKER.

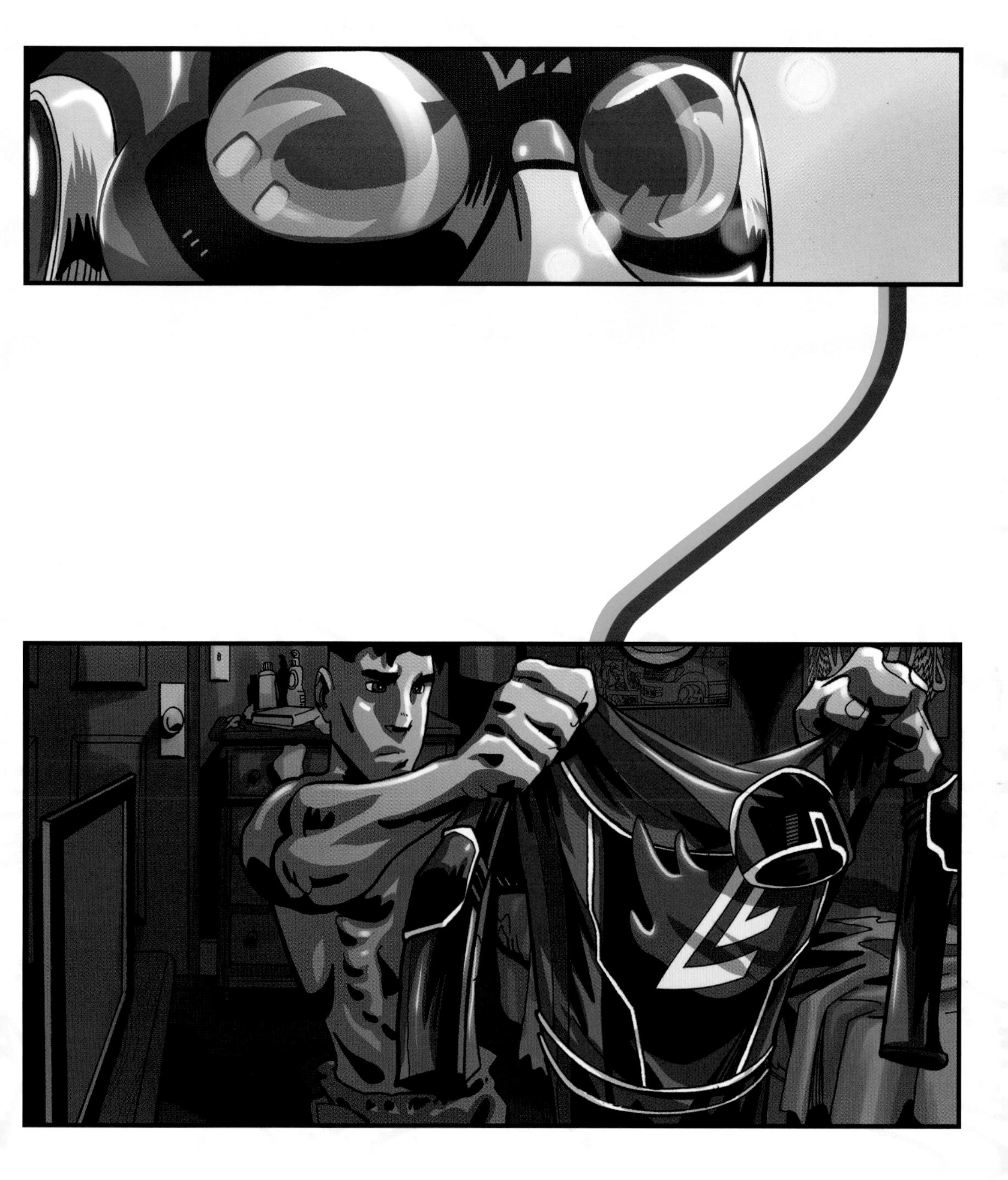

ACCELL™
THE EVENT
ACCELL

"Overture"

ONE YEAR AFTER THE EVENT

PLEASE... I'M BEGGING YOU...
SHOW ME...
...I HAVE TO KNOW...
--
--DAVID...
JONAH--
JONAH--!!

IT'S ALL RIGHT--
THEY'RE NOT HURTING ME--THEY CAN'T HURT ME!
YOU HAVE TO CALM DOWN--GO TO FLORIDA, LIKE I TAUGHT YOU!
JUST THINK ABOUT FLORIDA--
YEAH--
ZZZAAAPPP
--AND HERE'S SOME LUGGAGE TO TAKE WITH YOU--!!

ARRGGHHH--!!
WHAAAAMMM
JONAH--!!
YOU IDIOT--
--HE'S JUST A KID-- HE DOESN'T KNOW ANY BETTER--
JONAH--
--JONAH NO--!!
UH...
...UH...
...CRAP...

"La Dama en El Autobús"

ONE WEEK BEFORE THE EVENT

"HE HAS ALREADY SAVED $35. HIS GOAL IS TO HAVE ENOUGH MONEY SAVED IN SIX WEEKS TO PAY FOR THE BICYCLE.
SO, LET'S LOOK--
"--A QUARTIC TRINOMIAL IS A FOURTH-DEGREE POLYNOMIAL EXPRESSION CONTAINING THREE TERMS, YES?
"SO, IF 'W' REPRESENTS 'WEEKS,' THAT GIVES US '6W' WHICH NEEDS TO EQUAL 175, RIGHT?
"SO WE JUST NEED TO FACTOR IN THE 35 BUCKS IN HIS POCKET-- 35+6W=175.
"GET EVERYTHING ON ONE SIDE OF THE EQUATION AND THEN FACTOR THE QUADRATIC."
I STILL DON'T GET IT, MISS LORENA.
ME NEITHER.
IN ALGEBRA CLASS, I MOSTLY PERFECTED MY DOODLES OF SPIDER-MAN.
GO. ASK A REAL TEACHER.
THINK YOU COULD'VE SKIPPED THE BUS RIDE TODAY, LORIE.
I BUILT THIS SCHOOL, SHEP. FOR THEM. FOR THEIR FUTURE.
I PROMISED THAT EVERY DAY, I'D RIDE ALONG.

BESIDES, IF THIS MISSION GOES SIDEWAYS--
--HALF A DECADE IN THE MAKING--
--THEN I'VE *FAILED* THEM.
INDUSTRIAS FORESIGHT
...CAN'T BELIEVE WE'RE NOT ALLOWED IN CENTRAL CONTROL.
...BEEN PULLING ALL-NIGHTERS FOR *MONTHS*...
SHE'S BEEN RIDING US AROUND THE CLOCK--
--WE *DESERVE* TO BE THERE DURING THE *EVENT.*
AND WE'RE BANNED, LIKE LITTLE KIDS.
HELL, WE *MADE* THIS HAPPEN--
YEAH, I THINK LORENA'S KIND OF A BITCH, TOO.
NEVER SAYS "THANKS," NO "ATTABOYS."
THE DEVIL WEARS PRADA.
I-- UH--
--WE DIDN'T--
SURE YOU DID. LET'S HAVE IT.
TELL ME ABOUT *ME.*

WE'RE, UH--
--MS. PAYAN-- IT'S JUST THAT WE WORKED SO HARD--
--YOU FEEL YOU DESERVE TO BE PRESENT DURING THE EVENT.
YES...
YOU'RE RIGHT--
--BUT NOBODY EVER GETS WHAT THEY DESERVE.
BUZZ ALDRIN ACTUALLY BITCHED ABOUT NEIL ARMSTRONG BEING THE FIRST GUY OFF THE BOAT.
IT WAS ONE OF THOSE TREE-FOREST THINGS.
OUR PLANET DESERVES TO BE DESTROYED BY A GIANT HERSHEY'S KISS HURTLING THROUGH SPACE.
LET'S SEE IF WE CAN AVOID THAT.
YOU'RE MY GUYS.
CAN'T DO THIS WITHOUT YOU.
BUZZ ALDRIN...?
IT'S TRUE. SAW IT ON HBO.
DOUBT THOSE KIDS EVEN KNOW WHO THAT IS.
THEY THINK TONIGHT IS A NEW YEAR'S CELEBRATION... FOURTH OF JULY.
I DON'T WANT THEM IN CENTRAL CONTROL BECAUSE THEY SHOULD BE HOME WITH THEIR FOLKS.
THEY WON'T BE.
I KNOW. BUT IT WON'T BE BECAUSE I FORCED THEM TO BE HERE.

WE SHOULD BE DOING SOMETHING.
NO, YOU SHOULD EMPHATICALLY NOT BE DOING ANYTHING.
WE SHOULD BE PUSHING BUTTONS. IT'S WHAT ASTRONAUTS DO.
IT'S IN, LIKE, EVERY MOVIE.
"Monkeys"
FORESIGHT AMERICO LUNAR PLATFORM
ONE WEEK BEFORE THE EVENT
THOSE MOVIES ARE STUPID.
YOU'RE SITTING IN THE MOST ADVANCED FLYING MACHINE EVER BUILT BY THE HAND OF MAN.
OR WOMAN. OR NON-BINARY.
IT SHOULD BE AT LEAST AS SOPHISTICATED AS AN IPHONE.
"THERE ARE NO BUTTONS TO PUSH."
SP JAMILA PARKS
JUST BE THE MONKEY, JAMILA. YOU'RE JUST THERE TO HELP THE MACHINES.
YOU BE THE MONKEY.
ZOË--
XIAOHÁN. HSIAO-HAN.
--JUST RE-CHECKING ICARUS 2'S ORBIT SOLUTION--
NOT THIS AGAIN.
--ARECIBO IDENTIFIED ICARUS 2 SPECTROSCOPICALLY AS AN SQ TYPE--
--SIMILAR TO LL CHONDRITIC METEORITES.
THE ECHO OBTAINED AT GOLDSTONE REVEALED 0.75-SIGMA IN DOPPLER AND 0.57-SIGMA IN RANGE.
SP VALENTINA RESN

THOSE ARE STATISTICALLY SMALL VARIANCES, DR. BAKER.
DOES IT BOTHER ANYBODY ELSE THAT WE'RE LAUNCHING FROM AN ORBITAL PLATFORM--
--NAMED AFTER AN EXPLORER WHO CIRCLED THE NEW WORLD A DOZEN TIMES BUT NEVER FOUND IT--?
VESPUCCI WAS UNDERRATED...
THAT'S MY POINT, ZOË--
VESPUCCI--?
I MEAN, WHAT IF WE BUMP A CURB OUT THERE.
THEN I GUESS YOU'LL HAVE TO WING IT.
EXCUSE ME--?
GUESS, DR. BAKER. JUST KNOW THAT GOING MANUAL MIGHT KILL ELEVEN BILLION PEOPLE.
ZOË--
FOR CRYING OUT LOUD...
--THERE'S NO SPRITE UP HERE.
THERE'S SOMETHING CALLED "SIERRA MIST" BUT, YOU KNOW, WHAT THE HELL, ZOË?
SP DAVID POWELL
I SAY WE ABORT.
HOW ABOUT YOU, AL--?
AL--? AL--?!
SP MAJ ALISTAIR MEATH
COMING UP ON EVENT HORIZON, FOLKS--
MISSION CMDR EVAN CHESS
--HATE TO SPOIL THE FUN, BUT IF DR. BAKER CAN TOLERATE OUR BEING A FEW CENTIMETERS OFF--
--AND IF THE GOOD MAJOR IS THROUGH REVIEWING HIS LUNCH--
--LET'S GO TO MARS.
ICARUS 2 IS ONLY 216,924 MILES FROM LUNA, COMMANDER--
LET'S GO TO MARS ANYWAY.
MIGHT WANT TO WORK ON DEVELOPING A SENSE OF HUMOR, DR. BAKER.
WE'RE GOING TO BE FLYING TOGETHER FOR A WEEK BEFORE WE FIND THAT ROCK OUT THERE.
Who is Lorena Payan--?

GLOBAL **NOW**

LORENA

LESS THAN A YEAR AGO, RESEARCHERS AT THE WORLD-RENOWNED FORESIGHT CORPORATION IN CHIAPAS, MEXICO MADE AN ALARMING DISCOVERY.

AN ASTEROID THE SIZE OF HOUSTON, TEXAS ON A COLLISION COURSE WITH EARTH.

ONLY FORESIGHT'S ADVANCED, SOME CALL IT "FRINGE," SCIENCE HAS DEVELOPED A VIABLE PLAN TO SAVE MANKIND.

BUT WHAT DO WE REALLY KNOW ABOUT THIS CLOSELY-HELD MEXICAN CONGLOMERATE AND ITS CONTROVERSIAL CEO?

HOW THE FATE OF THE WORLD CAME TO REST IN HER HANDS

In less than ten years, Lorena Payan built the Foresight Corporation into a global titan through innovations in aerospace development, space exploration, and so-called "fringe" science.

A native of the impoverished Mexican state of Chiapas, Payan lost her mother at age twelve. She and her brother Ramon were raised by their paternal grandmother Isabel, while their father Enrique Payan attended M.I.T. in the United States.

Payan's father founded the Foresight Corporation in Silicon Valley when she was a teenager, using wealth accumulated from his various business ventures in Mexico.

After immigrating to America, Payan studied under the tutelage of the eminent physicist, Dr. Parker "Shep" Bingham, who has served as her mentor and most trusted advisor.

While Payan lived in America with her father, her brother returned to Mexico, where Ramon Payan rose within the political structure. While Enrique Payan planted himself and his daughter in the ground of the American Dream, Lorena's brother chose to fight for his people back home, to work within the system to pull Mexico out of corruption and save it from the drug cartels.

Ramon Payan inherited the leadership of Foresight upon their father's death and relocated the corporation's central office to Chiapas. The Payan siblings hired a near 100% Mexican labor force in every section of the company and revolutionized the local economy while bringing global attention to the plight of Chiapas's indigenous tribes and social conflicts. Lorena Payan assumed control of Foresight after her brother was killed in a car bombing.

SHEP, YOU'RE IN THE LADIES ROOM.
OF COURSE. THAT'S WHERE THE LADIES ARE.
YOU DO KNOW YOU HAVE A PRIVATE BATHROOM, YES?
WHAT THE HELL DIFFERENCE DOES IT MAKE.
GOTTA STAY STRONG FOR THE TROOPS.
THESE PEOPLE ARE NOT COMING BACK, SHEP.
THEY'RE NOT.
AND NOBODY CAN SAY FOR SURE OUR PLAN WILL ACTUALLY STOP THAT THING FROM HITTING EARTH.
I'M SENDING FIVE PEOPLE TO THEIR DEATH ON A HUNCH.
YAH.
THEY KNOW.
THEY WON'T EVER SAY IT, BUT THESE PEOPLE ARE TOO SMART NOT TO KNOW.
BULL$#!*ING OUR WAY THROUGH THIS IS THE WAY WE HONOR THEM.
ALL RIGHT, ZOË--
--LET'S GET 'EM TUCKED IN.
ROGER THAT, CONTROL.
T-MINUS TEN... NINE... EIGHT...

C'MON, ASTRID.
DAVID-- I'M SERIOUS!
EVENTUALLY, EVERYTHING WE FOCUS ON ABOUT OURSELVES WILL DETERIORATE.
OUR BODIES AND MINDS. WITH THEM, OUR SENSE OF REALITY AND STRENGTH OF EGO.
THE SEXIEST PARTS OF BOTH OF US WILL SUCCUMB TO TIME AND GRAVITY, MR. POWELL.
YOU KNOW HOW SHALLOW YOU SOUND?
I'M JUST BEING HONEST.
POINT IS, AT THE END OF IT ALL, WHEN WE'RE LIVING OFF SOFT FOODS AND TAKING TEN TRIPS TO THE BATHROOM A DAY--
--I'LL NEED SOMEONE AROUND TO MAKE ME LAUGH.
I'LL NEED **YOU**, DAVID.
SO PROMISE ME.
OKAY: I PROMISE I WON'T DIE.
UNTIL?
UNTIL WE'RE AT LEAST A HUNDRED AND TWENTY YEARS OLD.
"AND I'LL STILL LOVE YOU."
AND I'LL STILL LOVE YOU.
LIAR--
"--YOU'LL BE HITTING ON YOUR DAY NURSE..."
HOW'S THE WEATHER UP THERE, DOC...?
SP DAVID POWELL

"Icarus"

THIRTY MINUTES BEFORE THE EVENT

IF YOU WANT TO TALK, VAL.
OR IF YOU DON'T.
1962
1983
1984
1992
1995
1999
IT'S ALL RIGHT. THIS IS YOUR TIME.
BUT... SEEING AS HOW THIS MAY BE OUR LAST SESSION...
...I JUST WANT TO BE SURE YOU'RE NOT, FOR WHATEVER REASON...
...HOLDING BACK ANYTHING.
SHE SAID TO ME...
SHE *WHO?*
THE ONLY "WHO" THAT MATTERS HERE.
"YOU'RE THE ONLY PERSON I TRUST, OUT OF ALL THE SKILLED MINDS HERE, TO DO THIS THING," SHE TOLD ME.
KNOWING I HAVE NEVER DISAPPOINTED HER.
BECAUSE SHE AND I BOTH KNOW THE TRUTH, DOCTOR.
LIFE IS MADE UP OF A STRING OF ACCOMPLISHMENTS.
WHAT'S THIS?
THE YEARS.
THE YEARS WOMEN BEFORE ME DID AMAZING THINGS IN SPACE.
IF YOU ADD THEM ALL UP, THE NUMBER YOU'LL GET IS ***ZERO.***
UNLESS I DO THE ***IMPOSSIBLE--***
--AND PREVENT MY GIRLFRIEND, MY PARENTS, MY EX, YOU AND YOUR THREE HUNDRED DOLLAR HAIRCUT, AND EVERYONE ELSE...
"...FROM GOING THE WAY OF THE DINOSAUR."
1962
1983
1984
1992
1995
1999
2017!
SP VALENTINA RESNICK BAKER

"SUCCESS IS NOT FINAL, FAILURE IS NOT FATAL: IT IS THE COURAGE TO CONTINUE THAT COUNTS."
THOSE WERE CHURCHILL'S WORDS.
I SAY BOLLOCKS.
OUR GREAT UNION HAS KNOWN FAR TOO MANY FAILURES IN RECENT YEARS.
THE WORD HAS BECOME GLOBALLY ACCEPTABLE AS A BADGE OF HONOR FOR THOSE ON SOME MYTHIC QUEST FOR NOBLE GOALS.
WE WILL NOT ADOPT THIS WORD, MAJOR.
THERE WILL BE NO QUANTIFYING OF THE CHANCES FOR SUCCESS.
THE LIVES OF ALL OF HUMANITY HANG IN THE BALANCE.
YOU AND I SHALL SURELY HANG ALONG WITH THEM.
LET US THEN STARE DOWN THE DEVIL TOGETHER, MAJOR.
YES, PRIME MINISTER.
AFTER ALL, THE BEST ANY HERO CAN HOPE FOR...
"...IS A QUICK DEATH AND THE PILLOCKS GETTING THE LIKENESS RIGHT ON ONE'S STATUE."
SP MAJ ALISTAIR MEATH

AND WHY THE HELL DOES IT HAVE TO BE YOU, JAMILA?
30 IS SMART FIT BEAUTIFUL
IT DOESN'T, MOMMA.
MY CALL.
HAS IT EVER OCCURRED TO YOU THIS IS ALL PROPER?
MAYBE IT'S THIS WORLD'S TIME. THE LORD--
WILL OF THE FATHER?
THE MYSTERY OF HIS WILL.
WHAT ABOUT OUR WILL, MOMMA-- THE FREE WILL HE GAVE US?
ALONG WITH THE SENSE TO KNOW THOSE PEOPLE DON'T MIND SENDING YOUR BLACK ASS INTO SPACE, TO DIE FOR WHAT?
YOU'LL BE GONE. THEY'LL BE RIGHT HERE, CONTINUING TO DO WHAT THEY ALWAYS DO--
--VOTING REPUBLICAN.
WHICH IS WHY IT'S ON ME TO DO THIS.
OTHER PEOPLE NEED TO SEE THAT WE'LL CONTINUE TO FIGHT.
BEEN FIGHTING FOR A LONG TIME.
AND LOOK WHERE WE'RE AT.
"IN THE WORLD BUT NOT OF IT, BABY."
SP JAMILA PARKS

MY CHINA--?
BUD LIGHT.
ALL RIGHT, CHESS. YOU MAY CONTINUE TO LIVE.
42 PEOPLE ARE ABOUT TO COME THROUGH OUR FRONT DOOR. TRY NOT TO GLARE AT THEM.
I HATE PARTIES.
WHY I THREW ONE FOR YOU.
YOU'LL BE TRAINING ON THE LUNAR STATION FOR SIX MONTHS BEFORE YOUR MISSION EVEN BEGINS.
WHO KNOWS IF YOU'LL BE BACK FOR YOUR NEXT BIRTHDAY.
MY HUSBAND-- MISSION COMMANDER, TIME MAGAZINE MAN OF THE YEAR, SPACE COWBOY...
...AND ME, LITTLE OL' HOUSEWIFE... REVERSE COWGIRL...
CHESS, WHEN THE MEN INEVITABLY DRIFT TO THE STUDY TO WATCH FOOTBALL--
LET'S PLEASE REMIND THEM TO--

CHESS?!?

CHESS, COME IN!!

"Eleven Billion"

SIXTY SECONDS BEFORE THE EVENT

WINGING IT--

--?!?
ENCRYPTED LEVEL 12
Keep this off the air... |
...object disintegration at errant coordinates...
...collision with Foresight Americo imminent...
...JESUS...
...object fragments likely to survive re-entry... a grave risk to...

"The Beginning"

THE EVENT

"Clouds"

TWO WEEKS AFTER THE EVENT

A LITTLE ROUGH ON MARIKA, MAYBE?
NEED TO PUT A CORK IN THIS HERO WORSHIP, SHEP.
EVERYBODY TRYING TO SPIN ME... EVERYBODY TRYING TO FOX NEWS ME...
FOUND SOMETHING INTERESTING...
...OLD CLOUD DATA MANUALLY RECOVERED FROM A DEAD SERVER.
NEVER TRUSTED CLOUDS.
ONLY IDIOTS PUT THEIR BLIND FAITH IN SOME DAMNED "CLOUD" SOMEWHERE... STORE ALL THEIR PERSONAL DATA...
AND THAT'S WHAT WE'VE GOT HERE-- PERSONAL NOTES FROM SOME NIGHT TECH.
RANDOM BLOG ENTRIES... PORN... OLD FACEBOOK POSTS...
...TELEMETRY READINGS ON THE ICARUS ASTEROID.
OUTSIDE OF OUR SYSTEM...
...THESE READINGS DON'T LINE UP WITH OURS.
WELL, THERE'S A SHOCK.
READINGS OFF SOMEBODY'S BACKYARD TELESCOPE...
THESE READINGS ARE FROM ARECIBO.
AND HUBBLE.
I'VE KICKED THE TIRES ON THIS, LORIE. IF THESE NUMBERS ARE CORRECT--
--ICARUS WAS NEVER GOING TO IMPACT EARTH.

EVEN WEIRDER--
--EVERYBODY WHO EVEN MIGHT HAVE KNOWN THAT IS DEAD.
ASTRONOMERS KILLED IN CAR WRECKS... YOUNG TECHS OVERDOSING ON DESIGNER DRUGS.
MUGGINGS. ACCIDENTAL FALLS.
AS LUDICROUS AS IT SOUNDS--
--IT LOOKS LIKE MOST DATA ACCRUED SINCE WE DISCOVERED ICARUS FIVE YEARS AGO HAS BEEN COMPROMISED.
BOTS-- EXECUTIONABLE COMPUTER FILES--ALL BEARING THE SAME DIGITAL SIGNATURE, INFECTING DATA WORLDWIDE.
IT'S AS IF SOMEONE WANTED TO KEEP THIS TELEMETRY INFO SECRET.
OR, MORE SUCCINCTLY--
--WANTED FALSE TELEMETRY OUT THERE.
WANTED TO CONVINCE EVERYONE THE WORLD WAS ABOUT TO END--
--SO SHE COULD POSITION HERSELF AS THE ONLY PERSON WHO COULD "SAVE" US.
WHAT'S GOING ON, LORIE?
WHAT ON EARTH HAVE YOU DONE--?
SSSHNIKKT

MAINTENANCE--
--TO MY OFFICE. CODE SIX.
Miss Lorena--
Thank you for saving my Mommy and my cat, Dougie. I love you so much.
Billy

COVER
GALLERY

ACCELL

Art by Damion Scott, Robert Campanella, and Sigmund Torre

Art by Damion Scott, Robert Campanella, and Sigmund Torre

Art by Damion Scott, Robert Campanella, and Sigmund Torre

Art by Damion Scott, Robert Campanella, and Sigmund Torre
HDMI 4
ACCELL
100 POINTS
4
3
RCAM-SIG DUO
0110/17
Volume

Cover B Art by
Khary Randolph and
Emilio Lopez

Cover C Art by
John Cassaday and
Laura Martin

Cover D Art by
Phil Jimenez and
Romulo Fajardo, Jr.

Art by Keron Grant

Art by Patrick Zircher and Paul Mounts